TREES OF THE
AMERICAN SOUTHWEST

George A. Petrides

illustrations by Olivia Petrides

STACKPOLE
BOOKS

0 11557 03165 2

Published by
STACKPOLE BOOKS
5067 Ritter Road
Mechanicsburg, PA 17055
www.stackpolebooks.com

Printed in the United States of America

10 9 8 7 6 5 4 3 2 1

First edition

Originally published in 2000 by Explorer Press

Cover design by Wendy A. Reynolds
Illustrations on pages 6–8 reprinted from *A Field Guide to Western Trees*,
Houghton Mifflin Co., 1992
Maps on pages 108–109 based on Fowells (1965), Little (1971), and
MacMahon (1988)

Library of Congress Cataloging-in-Publication Data

Petrides, George A.
    Trees of the American southwest / George A. Petrides ; illustrations by
Olivia Petrides.—1st ed.
        p. cm. – (Trees of the U.S.)
    "Originally published in 2000 by Explorer Press"—T.p. verso.
    Includes biographical references (p.).
    ISBN 0-8117-3165-0 (pbk.)
    1.Trees—Southwestern states—Identification. 2. Trees—Southwestern
states—Pictorial works. I. Title. II. Series.

QK142.P48 2005
582.16'0979—dc22   2004058959

CONTENTS

FROM THE AUTHOR

I first became interested in the identification of trees and shrubs while studying the food preferences of deer during their critical winter season. It was important to identify not only the twigs browsed by deer but also those that the animals neglected or avoided as food. Even though leaves were absent, I had to identify these plants quickly while snowshoeing along cruise lines through the forest. Ever since then, I have tried to detect or confirm field marks that would easily identify a woody plant at any season, not just when flowers, fruits, or even leaves were present.

Acknowledgments

Dr. Leslie R. Landrum, Professor of Botany and Curator of the Herbarium, Arizona State University, generously reviewed major portions of the manuscript and made several helpful suggestions. Dr. Alan Prather, Curator, graciously made available the fine collection of Southwest plants that forms a part of the Michigan State University Herbarium. I am grateful, too, to Dr. Prather and to Dr. Stephen N. Stevenson, Associate Professor of Botany at Michigan State University, for suggesting improvements in the text.

My daughter, Olivia, Adjunct Professor at the School of the Art Institute of Chicago, provided the clear artwork for this book and others in this series. She also painted the color illustrations for our more comprehensive *Field Guide to Western Trees*. I wish to express my sincere appreciation to her for her fine work. Maria de los Angeles Calderoni of Pan American University, Edinburg, Texas; Dr. A. M. Powell of Sul Ross University, Alpine, Texas; and Geoffrey A. Levin of the Natural History Museum of San Diego, California, all advised on the pronunciation of Spanish names. Thomas Greensfelder, graphic artist, helped greatly to improve computerization.

An Important Note

There are indications in this book that fruits and other parts of certain plants reportedly have been used for food or medicinal purposes. Although this information has been gleaned from reputable sources, it is included here for general interest and has *not* been verified as being absolutely true. Do not eat or take internally any part of a plant for any purpose unless it has been confirmed by an expert that it is safe to do so.

As well, this book notes that some plants were once used to disable and catch fish—a practice that today is illegal and certainly unsportsmanlike.

GEOGRAPHIC SCOPE OF THIS BOOK

From southeastern California, through southern Nevada, Arizona, New Mexico, and west Texas, high mountain ranges alternate with deep canyons. Picturesque landscapes are everywhere. From snow-capped peaks to arid lowlands, the range of climates parallels that of the North American continent as a whole. In consequence, the natural vegetation extends from alpine tundra to desert scrub with forest and woodland in between. Unique species have evolved in the region in response to its varied environments.

The trees of the Southwest include a number of Mexican species that extend into the United States, mostly near the international border. Like the Mexican birds found there, these Mexican trees are of special interest to naturalists.

Arizona and New Mexico form the core areas of this book. Also included, however, are the Mohave and Sonoran desert regions of southeastern California and southern Nevada as well as that portion of western Texas—largely Chihuahuan desert— that lies south of New Mexico and includes the Big Bend National Park. The trees of these areas also occur in adjacent portions of Mexico. Our *Trees of the Rocky Mountains and Intermountain West* includes the desert species of this book, but more detailed treatment is given here.

HOW TO USE THIS BOOK

This book is designed for in-the-field use. It provides guidelines that will help the observer identify any tree that grows wild in the Southwest in any season, not just when the tree is in leaf or in flower. All 174 native or naturalized trees in the region are covered. These trees are divided into 42 small groups comprised of species that look alike whether or not they are actually related. Within each group, similarities and differences are pointed out.

The following chart (also shown on the book's back cover) will help you locate illustrations and information about the tree you are trying to identify. To use the chart, decide which statement 1 is true, then which statement 2 is true, and so on, until the appropriate section is reached.

1. Leaves needlelike or scalelike
   (conifers)   **Section I, Plates 1–7**
1. Leaves broad
   2. Leaves opposite or whorled
      3. Leaves compound   **Section II, Plates 8–10**
      3. Leaves simple   **Section III, Plates 11–12**
   2. Leaves alternate
      4. Leaves compound   **Section IV, Plates 13–20**
      4. Leaves simple   **Section V, Plates 21–39**
1. Yuccas, palms, cacti   **Section VI, Plates 40–42**

To use this chart, you must first be familiar with the meaning of some common descriptive terms, beginning with the difference between opposite, whorled, and alternate leaves. Opposite leaves occur in pairs, and the leaves are positioned directly across from each other on a twig. Whorled leaves are the same as opposite leaves, except there are three or more leaves ringing the twig. Alternate leaves are staggered along opposite sides of a twig; they are not directly across from each other. Remember that when leaves are absent, a specimen can still be categorized as alternate, whorled, or opposite by the positions of the leaf scars and buds.

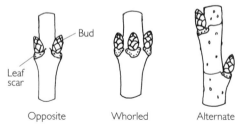

Opposite   Whorled   Alternate

The chart also differentiates between simple and compound leaves. A simple leaf has a single broad blade with a central midrib. The basal, or lowermost, portion of the midrib forms

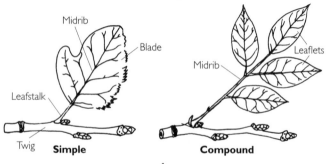

Simple   **Compound**

6

the leafstalk, which is attached to the twig. (The leafstalk is for the most part not woody and can be easily detached from the woody twig.) A compound leaf also has a midrib, but a number of separate leaflets are attached to it.

Compound leaves can be further identified as feather-compound, fan-compound, or twice-compound, according to the arrangement of the leaflets.

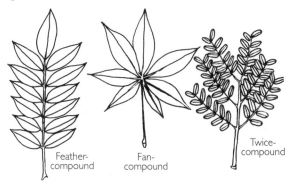

Feather-compound

Fan-compound

Twice-compound

When a leafstalk separates from the twig, it leaves a leaf scar that contains tiny dots, known as bundle scars, that can be seen easily with a hand lens; a bud also normally remains nearby. But when a leaflet becomes detached from a midrib only an indefinite mark of attachment is evident and no bud is present.

Bud

Bundle scar

Leaf scar

In this book, "twig" refers only to the end portion of a small branch, the part that constitutes the newest growth. A branchlet is the previous year's growth, separated from the twig by a series of encircling end-bud scars. "Branchlet" is also used here

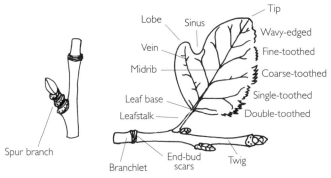

Tip

Lobe

Sinus

Wavy-edged

Vein

Fine-toothed

Midrib

Coarse-toothed

Single-toothed

Leaf base

Double-toothed

Leafstalk

Spur branch

Branchlet

End-bud scars

Twig

7

to mean any small branch that is not a twig. Short branchlets with closely positioned leaves and leaf scars are known as spur branches.

Other useful identifying features are the shape of the leaf edge; the number of bud scales and bundle scars; and the characteristics of the buds, pith, and leaf and stipule scars. The accompanying drawings illustrate these features.

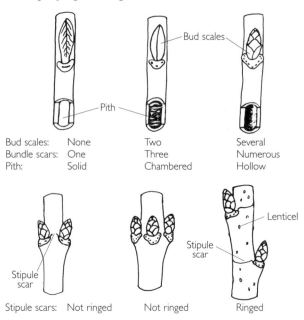

Bud scales:	None	Two	Several
Bundle scars:	One	Three	Numerous
Pith:	Solid	Chambered	Hollow

Stipule scars:	Not ringed	Not ringed	Ringed

This book follows the U.S. Forest Service definition of a tree: a woody plant at least 13 feet tall with a single trunk at least 3 inches in diameter at breast height. Trees not described as evergreen can be assumed to be deciduous. Within the text botanical terms are avoided; simple language is used throughout. Nevertheless, scientific as well as common names are given so that descriptions in other books can be compared.

Identifying Unknown Trees
Collecting plants for identification and study is a practice that has long been sanctioned by science. Collections should be made, however, only in moderation and under suitable conditions. Wild plant collection must be balanced against the need to preserve natural values. Also, remember that in some areas,

including national and state parks and monuments, it is illegal to collect plants without a permit.

Remember, too, that it is often easier to make an accurate identification in the field than it is to make one from a collected specimen. A number of important characteristics—milky sap, spicy odors, bark pattern, growth habits, and fallen leaves and fruits—are more obvious when you examine a whole living tree than they are when you look at a collected specimen.

If you do want to collect a specimen for later study and it is appropriate to do so, keep in mind that a good specimen is essential for correct identification. Avoid twisted, dwarfed, and gnarled branches. From a vigorous branch, clip from six inches to a foot of the branch tip so that both leaf and twig characteristics are present.

With the unknown tree or specimen at hand, use the chart to lead you to the proper section of this book, then scan the plates in that section to find the species that most resembles your tree. When leaves are absent, use the leafless key on pages 96–98 as well as the plate illustrations and text descriptions.

Fortunately, the field identification of trees requires a minimum of equipment: only a field guide and a hand lens are needed. A good hand lens is as essential to the botanical naturalist as binoculars are to the birder. Suitable hand lenses can be found at nature centers or any other place that sells optical equipment. A lens that magnifies 6x to 10x will not only disclose the beauty hidden in small blossoms but will be of great help in checking on the hairiness of leaves and twigs, the presence or absence of leafstalk glands, and other tiny details. Holding the lens close to your eye makes it almost part of you and usually enhances your field of vision.

Plant Names

In this book, common names that include the name of another unrelated group—Douglas-fir or Redcedar, for example—are either hyphenated or joined together to indicate that they are not true members of the group.

Although common names are well established for some species, such names often vary from one part of the country to another—and from one book to another. Because of this, scientific names are used to provide a standardized designation for a given species.

Scientific names have three essential parts: the name of the genus (plural *genera*), the name of the species (plural *species*), and the name, often abbreviated, of the botanist or botanists who assigned the name and stand as the authority behind it. Of the two Latinized terms, only the first name (the generic) is capitalized. An example is the scientific name for Pacific Dogwood: *Cornus nuttallii* Audubon.

Unfortunately, scientific names also may change as continued study indicates that a species is more closely related to members of a different group, that plants once thought to be two separate species should be combined as varieties of one species, or that a species originally thought to be new has already been named, and so forth.

Explaining the complicated rules of scientific nomenclature is beyond the scope of this book. To the amateur naturalist the principal value of scientific names is to ensure accuracy when seeking additional information about a species in other books. If both the Latin name and its authority agree, then the two books are presumably discussing the same species.

Scientific names tend to be anglicized when spoken. Don't hesitate to use them. In fact, if you call a certain plant an arbutus, a rhododendron, or a yucca you are already using scientific names. (In speech, the authority's names are usually omitted.)

The Flora of North America, now in development, is becoming the basic reference for plant names and classification. The scientific names accepted by the specialists who compiled the first volumes of *The Flora of North America* are used in this book.

For species not yet covered by that guide, two sources are utilized. For trees of the Southwest that also occur in California, the names of Hickman (1993) and his collaborators are adopted. For other species, the names listed are those of the developing Flora of Arizona (see Landrum, 1992–95) or of Little (1979). Full citations of these references are given in the References section. Unless markedly distinctive in the field (Arizona Pine or Lombardy Poplar, for example), varieties or subspecies are not emphasized here. For full citations of references, see page 98.

Measurements

Where appropriate in the text, measurements are given for tree height, leaf and bud size, and other characteristics. Trunk widths are for the diameter at breast height, commonly $4^{1}/_{2}$ feet above the ground, which foresters note as "d.b.h." Measurements are given in English units. For metric conversions, see page 109.

Environmental Factors

The aggregation of trees that occurs in any locality is determined first by the parent species present and then largely by the interacting factors of climate, soil, and other living things. Temperature and precipitation affect the survival of each tree species (especially that of seedlings) and also determine the characteristics of the soil upon which trees depend for much of their nutrient intake. Other plant and animal species may cause competition, disease, parasitism, browsing, and so on.

Differences in altitude cause climates, soils, and vegetation to vary greatly between locations. Tree floras in the mountains only a fraction of a mile apart may be quite different from each other and, in consequence, support different animal populations.

Plants that grow at low elevations in northern regions of North America are often found at high altitudes further south. A person ascending a high mountain may pass through several vegetative zones, each with its own characteristic tree species, before finally reaching timberline and alpine tundra near the top.

When you find and identify a tree that is new to you it is interesting to think about the environmental factors that enable its survival, and those that are likely limiting its distribution and abundance. Shallow soil, snow depth in winter, competition from other plants, excess soil moisture, drought, lack of soil fertility, fire, insect damage—all can keep a species from becoming more plentiful. Erosion, overuse, and pollution are human factors that can have powerful effects on a species' survival. As well, glacial or other geographic events might have brought the plant to its present distribution, or prevented its spread.

Exactly which environmental factors are affecting a specific tree cannot always be identified. Insight may come, however, as you examine other specimens at different locations. It is certain that some combination of climatic, soil, biotic, and historic factors has determined the current status of the species and will continue to influence its welfare.

I Trees with Leaves Needlelike or Scalelike Plates 1-7

1. PINES with FIVE NEEDLES PER BUNDLE

The white (or soft) pines typically have 5 blue-green *thin* needles per cluster, each bundle bound at the base by the 1/32"- 1/16" long remnant of a papery sheath. The cones, which drop early, are mostly slender, long-stalked, thin-scaled, and without prickles. Arizona Pine is an aberrant yellow pine with 5-needle clusters while Chihuahua Pine (Plate 3) is an unusual 3-needle white pine. Note the true cedars, bottom of text Plate 4, also with grouped needles.

COLORADO BRISTLECONE PINE *Pinus aristata* Engelm.
In contrast to most pines which display needles only on their twigs and nearby 2-4 year old branchlets, those of this species may be held for 10-17 years covering the branches in long, bushy foxtails. Needles are only 1"- 1 1/2" long, often with a sticky "dandruff" of tiny resin spheres. Cones 3"- 3 1/2" long, with slender, weak, 3/16"- 1/4" bristles. Seed 1/4"; wing ± 1/2" long. Found mainly at moderate to high elevations in Colorado and n. New Mexico, also nw. Arizona. Rocky Mountain Bristlecone Pine is another name. In the White Mountains of se. California, the related Intermountain (or Great Basin) Bristlecone Pine (*P. longaeva* Bailey) is thought be the world's oldest tree at about 5000 years. (Are aspens, Plate 25, older?)

SOUTHWESTERN WHITE PINE *Pinus strobiformis* Engelm.
A pine typical of the Southwest with needles *2 1/2"- 3"* long. Cones *short-stalked, 5"- 9"* in length, with scale tips *narrowed, bent back,* and *not* bristly. Seed 3/8"- 1/2"; wing *1/8"* long or less. Bark brownish. Height 60'- 80' (100'). Dry slopes at 6500'- 10,000' elevations from Arizona and New Mexico southward to cen. Mexico. Formerly named *P. reflexa* Engelm.

LIMBER PINE *Pinus flexilis* James
Needles much like Southwestern White Pine. Cones *3"- 6"* in length with scale tips *± squared.* Seeds red-brown, often *dark-mottled,* about 1/2" long, the wing 1/4" long or lacking. Presumably named for its flexible twigs, but those of some other western pines also can be twisted into knots. To 50' tall. Mainly in the Rockies, over wide elevations from cen. British Columbia to n-cen. New Mexico, n-cen. Arizona, and s. California.

ARIZONA PINE *Pinus ponderosa* var. *arizonica* (Engelm.) Shaw
Like typical Ponderosa Pine (Plate 2) but with *five* needles and cones only *2"- 3 1/2"* long. Some 2- and 3-needle clusters often present. Needle sheaths *long and persistent.* Height 80'- 100'. At 6000'- 8000', from se. Arizona /sw. New Mexico to nw. Mexico.

Plate 1

COLORADO
BRISTLECONE
PINE

LIMBER
PINE

SOUTHWESTERN
WHITE PINE

ARIZONA PINE

2. THREE-NEEDLE PINES

Pines with *three* needles per bundle, bundles mostly bound by a *long* and *persistent* basal sheath. Needles *over 2 1/2" long* and mostly moderately wide. Cones usually *short-stalked.* Most pines with 2 or 3 needles are termed *yellow* or *hard* pines but pinyon pines (Plate 3) and Chihuahua Pine are exceptions. Most yellow pines are useful for lumber, but the wood is pitch-filled and not as suitable for fine work as that of the *white* or *soft* pines (Plate 1). Native Americans ate pine seeds, used the pitch to waterproof woven containers, and made flour of the inner bark in hard times.

PONDEROSA PINE *Pinus ponderosa* Dougl.ex Lawson & Lawson

A large pine with 5"-10" needles and sheaths 1/2"- 1" long. Often two-needled. Cones egg-shaped, 3"- 6" long, with sharp tips or small prickles. Twigs moderately thick. The seed wing 1" in length. Young trunk dark, rough. Mature bark in yellow plates with flaky puzzlelike pieces. Height 60'- 130' (230'). Sunny sites at 4000'- 12,000' elevations mainly on dry soils. The most common, most economically important, and most widespread western conifer, the distribution of Ponderosa Pine is sometimes said to outline the American West. It often grows at lower elevations than other pines, forming pure or nearly pure stands with some ability to survive surface fires. Sooty grouse and red and gray squirrels eat the seeds; porcupines gnaw the inner bark; deer browse the twigs and needles. Not found until the 1930s, Washoe Pine (*P. washoensis* Mason & Stockwell) is similar but rare in the Sierra Nevada of w-cen. Nevada and e-cen. California. It has 4"- 6" needles, 2"- 3 1/2" cones, and a 1/2" seed wing.

APACHE PINE *Pinus engelmannii* Carr.

A tall pine with long needles in large clusters at the ends of *thumb-wide* twigs. Twigs appear *very* stout as seen against the sky. Needles (sometimes in 2s or 5s) are *8"- 15" long, drooping,* with *1"- 1 1/2"* sheaths. Cones *4"- 6"* in length, *prickly,* often persistent in twos and threes. Seed 5/16"; wing 1". Mature bark in yellow plates. Se. Arizona /sw. New Mexico to cen. Mexico.

CHIHUAHUA PINE

Pinus leiophylla var. *chihuahuana* (Engelm.) Shaw

Although this tree has clusters of only three needles, it is a member of the white pine (Plate 1) group. Needles are only *2 1/2"- 4"* long and, like those of most white pines, *thin* with *short* (1/32"- 1/16") basal sheaths. Twigs *slender.* Cones *1 1/2"- 3"* long, *long-stalked,* and *not* prickly; seed 1/8", wing 5/16". Unlike most white pines, cones may remain long on the tree and, unlike most other pines, stumps may sprout. Bark dark, furrowed. Height to 60'. Occurs at 5000'-7500' elevations from e-cen. Arizona /sw. New Mexico to cen. Mexico. The name, like that of the nearby Mexican state, is pronounced chee-WAH-wah.

Plate 2

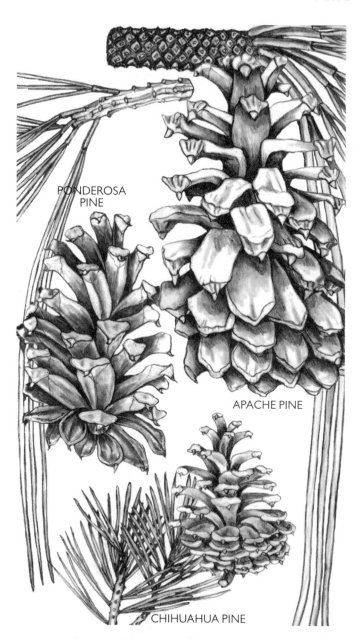

PONDEROSA
PINE

APACHE PINE

CHIHUAHUA PINE

3. PINYON (NUT) PINES

Pinyons are mostly short round-topped trees of the white pine group (Plate 1) that produce delicious nuts at the base of the cone scales. They have bundles of 1- 4 *stiff* and mostly *curved* needles *under 2 1/2"* in length and with *minimal* leaf sheaths. Cones stout, *less than 2 1/2"* wide, often nearly spherical, with scales *thick-edged* and mostly *thornless.* Nuts paired, 1/2"- 3/4" long, and *wingless.* Mainly on dry rocky sites.

Pinyon nuts formed a principal food of early Native Americans and are still much prized by people who find them before they are eaten by wild animals. They are especially good when roasted. As with other pines, Native Americans used the pitch to make watertight basketry. In Spanish, the name is spelled piñon.

With Singleleaf and Two-needle pinyons well-named, a nice set would be formed if Mexican Pinyon could be more widely known as Three-needle Pinyon and Parry Pinyon as Four-needle Pinyon.

SINGLELEAF PINYON *Pinus monophylla* Torr. & Frém.
  The *one* needle (rarely paired) is thick, *spine-tipped,* grayish, and 1"- 2 1/2" long. Cones *2"- 2 1/2"* long. The tree may reach 40' in height. Mainly at 4000'-6000' elevations from the Great Basin region (mainly Nevada) south to s. California and w. Arizona.

TWO-NEEDLE PINYON *Pinus edulis* Engelm.
  Needles *paired,* 3/4"- 2" long, dark green, sharp but *not* spiny. Cones *1"- 2"* in length. May grow to be 50' tall. Occurs at 4000'-7000' elevations from sw. Wyoming, Utah, and n-cen. Colorado to se. California, Arizona, New Mexico, and w. Texas. Reportedly sometimes single-needled in cen. Arizona and se. California.

MEXICAN PINYON *Pinus cembroides* Zucc.
  Clusters of *three needles* and cones are both *1"- 2 1/2"* in length. Trunk is gray-brown, furrowed. Found at altitudes of 5000'-7000' in se. Arizona /sw. New Mexico and from w-cen. Texas south to cen. Mexico. Sometimes called Three-needle Pinyon.

PARRY PINYON *Pinus quadrifolia* Parl. ex Sudw.
  A localized nut pine with (3-) *4-leaved,* yellow-green needle clusters. Leaves 1" –1 1/2" long; cones 1 1/2"– 2 1/2" in length, sometimes with a small prickle. Trunk gray to brown and scaly. Height 15–30 ft. Dry slopes at 4000'–6000' elevations in sw. California (Riverside and San Diego counties) and Baja California Norte.

16

Plate 3

SINGLELEAF
PINYON

TWO-NEEDLE
PINYON

NUT

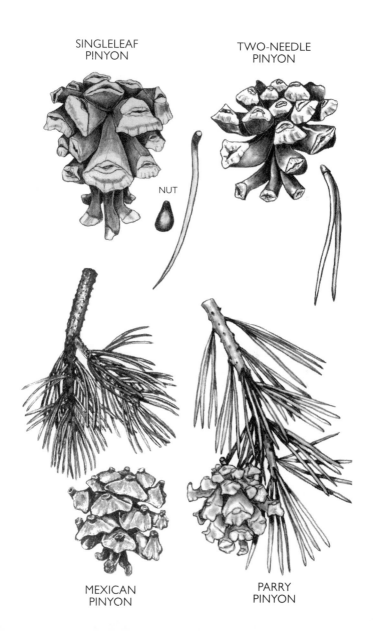

MEXICAN
PINYON

PARRY
PINYON

4. NEEDLES on WOODY PEGS: Spruces

Spruces have needles *single* on *small, stout, woody pegs* (seen best on dead twigs /branchlets). Unlike the flat, blunt needles of true firs and Douglas-fir (Plate 5), spruces of the Rocky Mountains have *4-sided, pointed* needles that grow all around the twigs and twirl easily between the fingers. Spruce twigs are hairy or not (remove needles and use lens). Cones brown and woody. Cone scales *papery, not* prickly and, in our species, with *ragged* tips. Trunk bark brown and *scaly*. Southwest spruces occur mainly above 8000'.

Several species are used in landscaping. Spruce wood is soft, light, straight-grained, and useful for many purposes. It is a principal source of pulp for making paper. Spruce needles drop quickly .upon drying, reducing the value of these species as Christmas trees. In bad times, early settlers ground the inner bark of spruces and added it to flour. Spruce beer reportedly can be made from fermented needles and twigs boiled with honey.

ENGELMANN SPRUCE *Picea engelmannii* Parry ex Engelm.
The principal spruce of the Rocky Mountains, growing south from cen. British Columbia to high elevations in the mountains of Arizona and New Mexico. Needles are about 1" long, dark- to blue-green, ± flexible, and only *moderately* sharp. Twigs mostly *hairy*. Cones *1/2"- 2" (3")* long. Height 80'- 100' (180'). A major lumber tree, sometimes with resonant logs. George Engelmann was a 19th century physician and botanist.

BLUE SPRUCE *Picea pungens* Engelm.
A species much like Engelmann Spruce (Plate 6) and often difficult to distinguish from it. Foliage is green to blue-green, seldom as markedly blue as cultivated varieties. Needles are stiff and *sharp*, twigs are *hairless*, and cones are 2"- 4" long. The trunk bark tends to be *darker* and thicker than that of Engelmann Spruce. Mostly cen. Rockies; at high altitudes in the Southwest. State tree of Utah and Colorado.

Note from Plate 1: **TRUE CEDARS** (*Cedrus* species) are pinelike imported trees frequently planted in areas of moderate climate. The evergreen needles are not tied in bundles like pines but grow mostly in clusters on stubby *spur branches*. The brown, woody cones, often called wood-roses, soon *shed* their scales. **Atlas Cedar** (*C. atlantica* Manetti) of North Africa has needles *1/2"- 1"* long, branchlets *not* drooping, twigs *hairy,* cones 2"- 3" wide with scale tips *square*. **Deodar Cedar** (*C. deodara* Loud.) of the Himalayas has foliage *1"- 2"* in length, branchlets *drooping,* twigs *hairy,* cones *3"-5"* wide with scale tips *rounded*, and leader *may* lean. **Cedar of Lebanon** (*C. libani* Loud.) has cones of similar size but needles *1"- 1 1/4"* long, twigs *hairless,* and branchlets *not* drooping.

Plate 4

ENGELMANN
SPRUCE

BLUE
SPRUCE

X-SECTION OF
NEEDLE

TRUE
CEDARS

ATLAS
CEDAR

DEODAR
CEDAR

TYPICAL CONE OF
TRUE CEDAR

CEDAR OF
LEBANON

5. CONIFERS with FLAT NEEDLES

These trees have needles *flat, blunt,* mostly *white-banded* beneath, and in *flat sprays.* Plucked twigs show *smooth circular* leaf scars. True firs *(Abies)* have *stout* needle bases, *blunt* buds, and *upright* cones whose *thick, fleshy* scales *soon fall apart.* Douglas-fir has *narrow,* almost hairlike, needle bases as well as *pointed* buds and *pendent, brown* cones with *thin, woody, persistent* scales.

WHITE FIR *Abies concolor* (Gord. & Glend.)Lindl.
A fir of low and middle elevations with foliage in *flat sprays* but ± *curved upward in a shallow U-shape.* Needles are *blue-green,* ± *white-powdered,* and *1 1/2"- 2 1/2" (3")* long. They have *rounded* tips, two *pale green lines* beneath, and are often *narrowed* at the base. Cones *green,* 3"- 5" long. Height 100'- 180' (210'). Occurs from Washington and se. Idaho to n. Mexico. The specific name *concolor* refers to the uniform color of the needles. In Europe, plantings are often called Concolor Fir. The odorless wood was once in demand for butter tubs and cheese molds.

ROCKY MOUNTAINS SUBALPINE FIR *Abies bifolia* Murray
A tree of cold climates and high elevations, from sea level in the far north to near timberline in mountains of the Southwest. The very narrow *steeplelike* crown, though seen in other firs (and spruces), is typical. Needles 3/4"- 1 1/2" long, whitened *both above and beneath,* with a *single* white stripe above. Needle tips rounded or notched. Twigs sometimes slightly hairy. Bark hard, gray. Mature cones *purplish,* 2 1/2"- 4" long. Height 20'- 100' (130'). In the Rockies, occurs from s-cen. Alaska and cen. Yukon to New Mexico /Arizona. Often reproduces by layering where branches in contact with the ground take root. Once called Alpine Fir, botanists now tend to restrict the term alpine to tundra vegetation growing above timberline. Corkbark Fir [var. *arizonica* (Merriam) Lemmon] has soft whitish bark and ranges south from s. Colorado. Trees of coastal regions, with minor distinctions, retain the former name *A. lasiocarpa* (Hook.) Nutt.

COMMON DOUGLAS-FIR *Pseudotsuga menziesii* (Mirb.) Franco
Best field marks are twigs that *droop* markedly and unique *3-pointed bracts* that protrude well beyond the cone scales (cones usually abundant beneath the tree). Needles 3/4"- 1 1/2" long and *thin-stalked.* Cones 2"- 3 1/4" in length. Trunk bark dark and grooved. Height 80'- 100' (300'). An important lumber tree. Found throughout the western mountains; mostly above 9000 feet in the Southwest. Named for David Douglas an early Scottish botanist, but found by Archibald Menzies one of Douglas' countrymen. False-hemlock meaning of *Pseudotsuga* could be an alternate common name. Bigcone Douglas-fir [*P. macrocarpa* (Vasey) Mayr] occurs in s. California mountains.

Plate 5

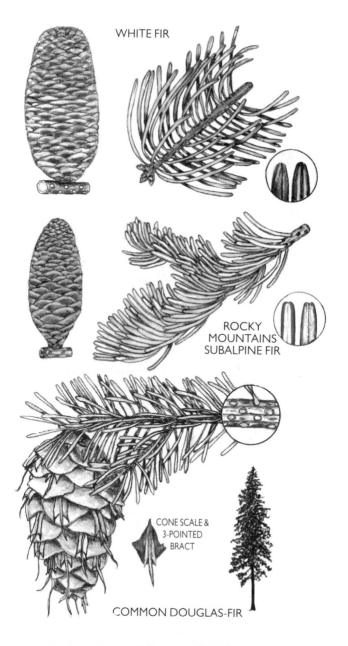

WHITE FIR

ROCKY
MOUNTAINS
SUBALPINE FIR

CONE SCALE &
3-POINTED
BRACT

COMMON DOUGLAS-FIR

6. CONIFERS with SCALELIKE FOLIAGE: CYPRESSES and JUNIPERS I

In the Southwest, most trees with small *scalelike* leaves are either cypresses or junipers. Species of these groups look much alike. The scaly leaves are *under 1/4"* long, mostly *gland-dotted* (use lens), and often *aromatic.* Scale-covered twigs are *mostly 4-sided,* 1/32"- 1/16" thick, and *not* in flat sprays. Trees are generally under 40' tall and grow mostly on dry sites. Only one cypress (and its variety) occurs in our area, but there are many junipers (below and Plate 7).

CYPRESSES, unlike junipers, display *only* scalelike leaves. Their cones are *brown, spherical,* and *woody.* The cones are mainly *inedible* and, with both sexes on the *same* tree, are *usually present.* Cypress bark is tight and of no particular value (see junipers).

ARIZONA CYPRESS *Cupressus arizonica* Greene
This, the only native cypress in our area, has 4-sided twigs that *branch at wide angles.* Leaf scales are blue- or pale-green and about 1/16" long. Cones are ball-shaped, *6-8 scaled,* and 3/4"- 1 1/4" in diameter. Trunk bark, typically, is *rough, dark,* and *furrowed.* Height 40'- 70'. Near the international border from se. Arizona to w. Texas and south into Mexico at 3500'-9000' elevations. Also in s-cen. California. A variety with smooth reddish bark is sometimes separated as *C. glabra* Sudw. and called Smooth Cypress.

JUNIPERS have mainly scalelike foliage but *also* tend to display small, sharp, *awl-shaped* needles, especially near the twig tips. The fruits of junipers (considered to be cones with fused scales) are unlike those of cypresses. They are *hard-fleshy, berrylike,* mostly 1/4"- 1/2" in diameter, *either* blue or red-brown when mature (often with a whitish powder), and 1- to many-seeded.The berries mature over either one or two years and thus fruits of either *one or two sizes* are present. They fall when ripe, are frequently consumed by wildlife (they were also eaten by Native Americans and early settlers), and are present only on *female* trees. They are *not,* therefore, always at hand. The bark of most junipers is shreddy and, when dried, good for starting fires. Junipers occur mainly at elevations between 4500' and 6500'. See Junipers II, Plate 7.

Tamarisks (*Tamarix* spp.) are imported trees with tiny *true* flowers, scaly and *juniperlike* but *non-glandular* leaves, and *rounded* twigs. Athel Tamarisk [*T. aphylla* {L.} Karst.] is densely evergreen; the *deciduous* French Tamarisk (*T. gallica* L.) is a weed in some areas.

Plate 6

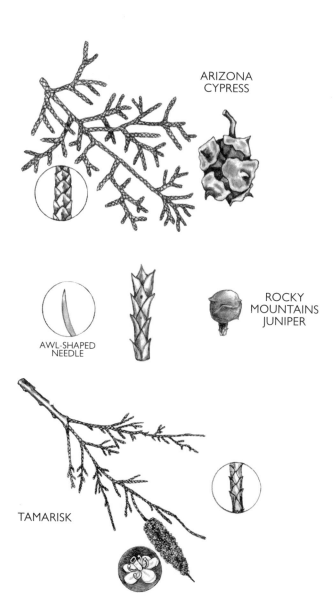

ARIZONA CYPRESS

AWL-SHAPED NEEDLE

ROCKY MOUNTAINS JUNIPER

TAMARISK

7. FOLIAGE SCALELIKE: JUNIPERS II

Among junipers in the Southwest, four principal species are widespread especially in Arizona. The Mexican border species listed here have more restricted ranges, mainly in California and Texas. An additional species, Common Juniper (*J. communis* L.), *lacks* scaly leaves and has only *hollowed, whitened,* awl-like needles in *whorls of three.* It is local in northern districts and *seldom* attains tree size. For general characteristics /distinctions from cypresses, see Plate 6.

ROCKY MOUNTAIN JUNIPER *Juniperus scopulorum* Sarg.
A widespread juniper with twigs ± *threadlike* (only about 1/32" thick), ± 4-sided, and *drooping.* Leaf scales bluish to *dark* green, ± *long-pointed,* usually with a gland. Mature fruits *blue, juicy,* mainly *2-seeded,* and of *two* sizes. From e-cen. British Columbia to Arizona and New Mexico. Bighorn sheep browse the twigs.

ONE-SEED JUNIPER *Juniperus monosperma* (Engelm.) Sarg.
Ranging from s. Utah and s. Colorado to cen. Mexico, this tree is similar to the last but has leaves *gray-green,* twigs ± *1/16"* thick, and fruits of *one-size,* mostly *single-seeded.* Berries are eaten by Gambel quail, gray foxes, raccoons, and rodents.

UTAH JUNIPER *Juniperus osteosperma* (Torr.) Little
A juniper with leaves *yellow-green, short-pointed,* and *lacking* gland dots. Mature fruits are dry, *red-brown,* of *either* 1 or 2 sizes, and with *one* (rarely two) seeds. It occurs from se. Idaho and s. Montana to Arizona and nw. New Mexico. Said to be the most common tree in Utah and Nevada.

ALLIGATOR JUNIPER *Juniperus deppeana* Steud.
Also red-fruited, this tree has a *checkered* trunk that resembles an alligator's hide. Leaf scales blue-green, *long-pointed,* and *glandular.* Fruits of *two* sizes; seeds 3-6. Wild turkeys and various mammals eat the fruits; deer browse the twigs. Ranging from cen. Arizona, cen. New Mexico, and w. Texas south into Mexico. Ferdinand Deppe was a 19th century German botanist.

Junipers that range near the Mexican border mostly have leaf glands *present* plus mature fruits *reddish,* of *one* size, and with *1* (-2) seed(s). **California Juniper** (*J. californica* Carr.), with *blunt* leaves and *shreddy* bark, is found on coastal slopes and inland to w. Arizona. **Roseberry Juniper** [*J. coahuilensis* (Mart.) Gaus.] occurs south from s. Arizona and w. Texas with leaf scales *spreading* and twigs *angled.* **Pinchot Juniper** (*J. pinchotii* Sudw.) ranges from se. New Mexico and sw. Texas north to n. Texas and sw. Oklahoma with *long-pointed* leaves and *furrowed* bark. **Weeping Juniper** (*J. flaccida* Schlecht.) of sw. Texas and nearby Mexico has branches *strongly drooping* and fruits with *4-15* seeds.

Plate 7

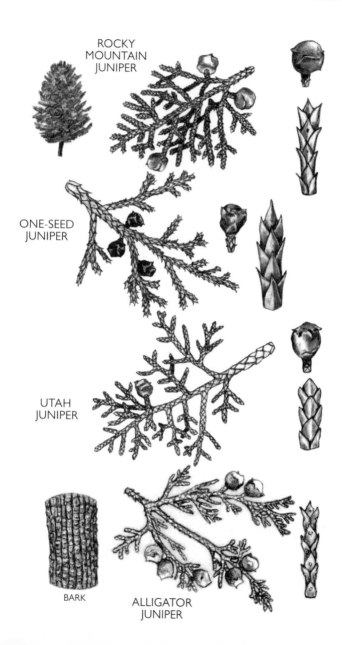

ROCKY
MOUNTAIN
JUNIPER

ONE-SEED
JUNIPER

UTAH
JUNIPER

BARK

ALLIGATOR
JUNIPER

II. Trees with Opposite Compound Leaves
Plates 8-10

In contrast to the needleleaf species of Plates 1-7, most other trees in the Southwest are *broadleaf* plants with either compound or simple foliage. Forty-four trees of the region have *compound* leaves. The nine species of this section have *opposite* compound foliage while the 35 trees of Section IV (Plates 13-20) have *alternate* compound leafage. *Be sure not to mistake the leaflets of a compound leaf for the blades of simple leaves* (see Figure 1, page 8). After leaves have fallen, the bare twigs of all opposite-leaved species (Plates 8-12) may need to be compared. See also the Key to Trees in Leafless Condition (pp. 96-98). Some trees have spur branches crowded with leaf scars (Figure 2, page 9). Though sometimes such leaf scars appear to be opposite, of our opposite-leaved species only Desert-olive Forestiera (Plate 12) has spur branches.

8. LEAFLETS w/ UNEVEN BASES: Elderberries

Unlike the trees of Plates 9-10, elderberries are trees or shrubs whose leaflets have *uneven* bases and twigs that are thick but *weak*, containing *wide* pith. Buds *obviously* scaly, a central terminal bud *lacking,* and *lines* connect the paired leaf scars. Bundle scars 3-7. Tiny, white, summer flowers and *small, juicy, several-seeded* fruits in ± *flat-topped* twig-end clusters 2"- 8" across. The blue to black fruits may have a *whitish coating.* Though reported to contain hydrocyanic acid, the fruits are often cooked into jam or jelly. The two species are often combined as varieties of *S. mexicana* Presl.

BLUE ELDERBERRY *Sambucus caerulea* Raf.
A widespread western elderberry. Leaves 5"- 8" long with *3-9* short- to *long-pointed* leaflets. Leaflets *2"- 6"* in length, *hairless,* and mostly *fine-toothed.* Side leaflets have stalks *1/4"- 1/2"* long. The dark but white-powdered fruits display a beautiful *sky-blue* color. Though mostly shrubby, some plants become 25' tall. From s. British Columbia to n. Mexico at elevations to 10,000'.

VELVET ELDERBERRY *Sambucus velutina* Durand & Hilgard
Found in California east to w-cen. Nevada and nw. Arizona, this elderberry has leaves with only *3-5* leaflets. Leaflets *short-pointed, velvet-hairy, fine-toothed,* and only *1"- 3"* long. Stalks of side leaflets are *lacking* or under 3/16" long. Fruits *blackish.* To 20' tall on slopes at 3000'-8000' elevations. Native Americans often favored this species in making fires. They used a dry half-inch branch as a spindle, spinning the wood between their hands. The base of the spindle, or drill, was surrounded by shredded tinder and forced into a small pit in a flat piece of dry cottonwood or juniper root. The spindle was rotated rapidly until friction caused smoke and, finally, flame to ensue.

Plate 8

FRUITS

FLOWERS

BLUE ELDERBERRY

VELVET ELDERBERRY

9. LEAFLET BASES EVEN:
Ashes I and Ashleaf Maple

Ash leaves are mostly 8"-12" long with 3-9 (13) leaflets *fine-toothed* or smooth-edged and bases *even*. Buds are rounded, mostly brown with a smooth -granular surface, the central end bud *present*. Leaf scars shield-shaped with *many* bundle scars (use lens). Twigs *strong* with pith *narrow* and mostly opposite-branched. Flowers small, dark, *clustered,* mostly *without* petals, in early spring usually ahead of the leaves. Fruits small, *dry,* one-seeded, the *single* wing like the blade of a tiny canoe paddle. Trunk mostly gray, *fine-fissured.* Heights 60'- 80'. See also footnote Plate 10 and Singleleaf Ash, Plate 12. Ashleaf Maple is not related but has large opposite leaves, usually *trifoliate* in the West, that somewhat resemble those of ashes. Western Mountain Maple (Plate 11) may have some 3-leaflet foliage.

VELVET ASH *Fraxinus velutina* Torr.

Leaves *4"- 6"* in length, the 3-5 leaflets *long-pointed* at both ends, *wavy-toothed* near the tip, and sometimes *hairy* beneath. Leaflet stalks *1/8"- 1/4"* long. Twigs hairless or *long-hairy.* Fruit *1/2"- 1 1/4"* in length, the wing about as long as the *plump* seed. Height to 40'. Distributed from s. Nevada and sw. Utah across Arizona to s. New Mexico and n. Mexico.

FRAGRANT ASH *Fraxinus cuspidata* Torr.

This, the only *white-flowered* ash in the region, is found from Mexico north to n. Arizona and s-cen. Texas. Leaves 3"- 6" long with 3–7 leaflets each 1 1/2"- 3" in length, *hairless,* usually *sharply* toothed and *long-pointed,* the stalks *more than* 1/4" long. Twigs hairless; buds sticky. Flowers in drooping clusters, 4-petaled, *fragrant.* Fruit 3/4"– 1 1/4" long and winged *to the base* of the *flat* seed. Rarely to 20 ft. tall. Dry slopes.

LOWELL ASH *Fraxinus lowellii* Sarg.

Reported only from n. and cen. Arizona, with twigs *hairless* and *4-lined* or 4-angled. Leaves *3"-6"* long with 3-7 ± *stalkless, egg-shaped,* and ± leathery leaflets. Fruit 3/4"-1 1/4"; seed *flat.*

ASHLEAF MAPLE (BOX-ELDER) *Acer negundo* L.

Unlike ashes, the leaf teeth are *large and coarse* (occasionally none). Twigs green or purple, leaf scars *narrow* and *meeting in raised points,* bundle scars *3* (-5), buds *white-hairy,* flowers *green*; and fruits *paired* maple "keys" (see Plate 11). Trunk bark *dark.* Height 50'- 70'. An eastern tree ranging west to w. Alberta /nw. Montana and across the Southwest The only regional maple always with compound leaves. The sap can be made into syrup. Wood is used for boxes but the tree is not related to elders. Foliage resembles Poison-oak [*Toxicodendron diversilobum* (Torr. & Gray) Greene] but that shrub /vine has leaves alternate.

Plate 9

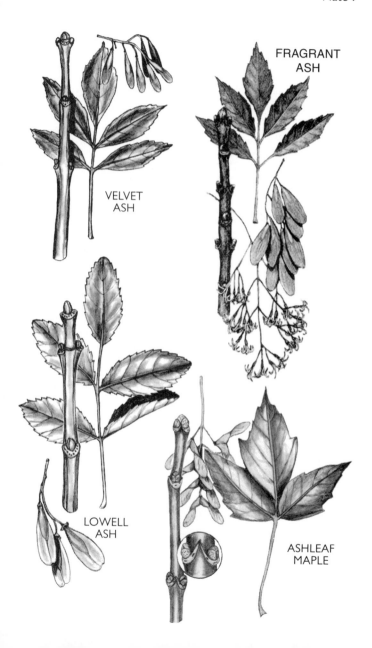

FRAGRANT
ASH

VELVET
ASH

LOWELL
ASH

ASHLEAF
MAPLE

10. LEAFLET BASES EVEN: Ashes II

The ashes of Plate 9 have 3"- 6" leaves and leaflets often long-pointed. They are distributed over areas well northward of the Mexican boundary as well as (except for Lowell Ash) near the border. The ashes of this plate, on the other hand, have mostly smaller leaves, short-pointed or blunt leaflets, and occupy only rather limited ranges in the United States. Fresno is Spanish for ash.

CHIHUAHUA ASH *Fraxinus papillosa* Lingelsh.
An essentially-Mexican ash that ranges north from the mountains of Sonora and Chihuahua in n. Mexico to reach se. Arizona, sw. New Mexico and w. Texas. Leaves *3"- 6"* long with 5-9 leaflets each 1 1/2"- 2 1/2" long, *whitish* beneath, *stalkless,* and with fine teeth or none. Twigs *hairless.* Fruit 1"–1/4" in length with wing *blunt,* and seed *flattened.* Height to 20'. Rocky slopes. The name of the Mexican state and of this ash is pronounced chee-WAH-wah.

GOODDING ASH *Fraxinus gooddingii* Little
A small-leaved shrub or small tree known only from the mountains of se. Ariz. and nearby Sonora, Mexico. Leaves only *1"– 3 1/4"* long with 5–9 *(mostly 7),* leaflets each 3/8"–1" long, often *partly fine-toothed,* and sometimes ± leathery. Leafstalks *narrowly winged* (use lens). Twigs and leaflet undersides somewhat *brown-hairy.* Fruit 1/2"– 1" long, the wing broad, *blunt,* and seed *flattened.* Height to 20'. Rocky slopes and ridges. The Peña Blanco and Sycamore Canyon areas in the Coronado National Forest west of Nogales, Arizona, are sites for this ash. The tree is named for Leslie N. Goodding, an American botanist who discovered it in 1934.

GREGG ASH *Fraxinus greggii* Gray
Found in sw. Texas and n. Mexico, this small ash has leaves *1"- 2 1/2"* in length with stalks *winged* (use lens). The 3-7 leaflets are 1/2"–1 1/4" long, *hairless,* sometimes *wavy-toothed,* often ± leathery, and with tips somewhat *rounded.* Twigs hairless or slightly *gray-hairy.* Fruits 1/2"– 3/4" long, the wing *narrowed* at the tip, and seed *plump.* Height to 20 ft. Rocky soils, Big Bend National Park to Del Rio, Texas, and over much of ne. Mexico. Josiah Gregg of Independence, Mo., was active in the region as a trader, author, and botanist during the early 19th century

---

Additional tree of Plate 9 - **European Ash** (*F. excelsior* L.), sometimes planted, has leaflets 7-13 and buds *black.*

Plate 10

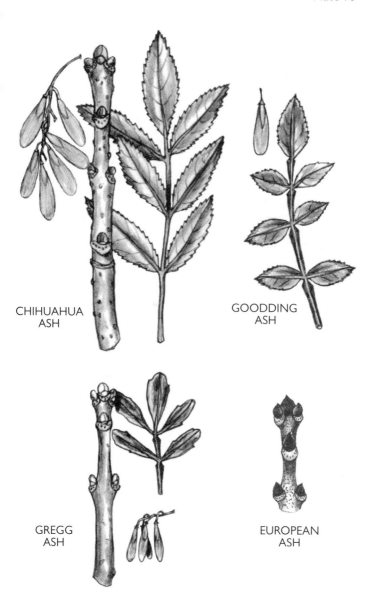

CHIHUAHUA
ASH

GOODDING
ASH

GREGG
ASH

EUROPEAN
ASH

III. Trees with Opposite Simple Leaves
Plates 11-12

Trees with opposite leaves are much fewer than those with alternate foliage (Sections IV-V). While species with opposite compound leafage comprised Section II (Plates 8-10), the seven trees in our area with opposite simple leaves are covered in this Section. When leafless, plates of all trees with opposite leaf scars (Plates 8-12) must be compared. Desert-willow of Plate 33 and the buckthorns of Plates 36 and 38 may have some leaves opposite.

11. OPPOSITE LEAVES FAN-LOBED: Maples

The only trees in the Southwest with opposite *lobed* foliage are maples, and only they have the *paired, dry, winged* fruits called *keys* (for Ashleaf Maple, see Plate 9).The leafstalks of maples are *long*, twigs are *slender* and mostly red-brown, buds are *pointed*, bundle scars are *three,* and flowers are in *umbrella-shaped* groups. Autumn foliage is colorful and springtime sap can be boiled into a sweet syrup. Maples sometimes attain a height of 40'. Arizona Sycamore and California Fremontia (Plate 23) as well as White Poplar (Plate 25) have *alternate* leaves maplelike.

WESTERN MOUNTAIN MAPLE *Acer glabrum* Torr.
  A shrub or small tree with leaves *4"- 7"* long and *3-5* lobed, with leaf teeth small, *many,* and *sharp*. Foliage sometimes divided into *three coarse-toothed leaflets*. Buds with only *two* scales. Flowers May-July. Each fruit *3/4"- 1"* long; the paired fruit *angled* at about 45°, August-September. Distributed throughout the western mountains from se. Alaska and e-cen. British Columbia to n. Mexico. Also known as Rocky Mountain Maple and Douglas Maple. Twigs are browsed by deer, mountain sheep, and cottontail rabbits; seeds are eaten by squirrels and many kinds of birds. In winter, dogwoods (Plate 12) also show two bud scales but twig leaf scars are raised and fruits are fleshy.

CANYON MAPLE *Acer grandidentatum* Nutt.
  A small-foliaged maple with leaves *2"- 4 1/2"* long and equally wide. Leaf teeth large, relatively *few,* widely-spaced, and *rounded.* Buds mostly *4-scaled*. Flowers April-May. Single fruits 1/2"- 1" long, in *U-shaped* pairs, June-September. A tree of the Rocky Mountains, ranging from s-cen. Montana, se. Idaho, and w. Wyoming to se. Arizona, s-cen. Texas, and Mexico. Also known as Bigtooth Maple, a translation of the scientific name. Sometimes tapped for its sweet sap and called Sugar Maple, but that name is better reserved for the eastern *A. saccharum* Marsh. that yields the maple sugar and maple syrup of commerce (two of the few foods native to North America).

Plate 11

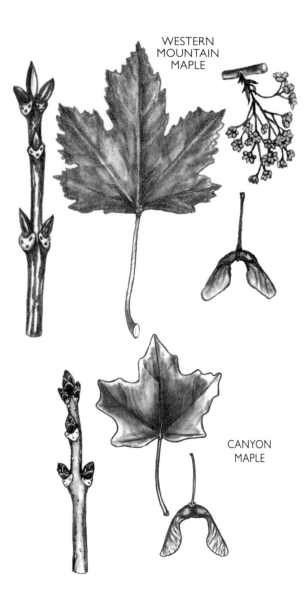

WESTERN
MOUNTAIN
MAPLE

CANYON
MAPLE

12. OPPOSITE LEAVES NOT LOBED

The first species has leaves mostly toothed; the others lack dentition.

SINGLELEAF ASH *Fraxinus anomala* S. Watson
An unusual ash, mainly with only *one* leaflet (occasionally 2-3). Leaflet 2"- 3" long, hairless, often *almost circular,* with small, *blunt* teeth or none. Twigs *4-lined* or 4-angled; bundle scars *many.* Flowers tiny, greenish, *lacking* petals, spring. Fruits dry 1/2"- 3/4" long, seed flattened, winged to the base, summer. Mountains, from Utah and w. Colorado to se. California and s. Arizona. Common in Zion and Grand Canyon national parks. Lowell Ash (Plate 9) also has 4-lined twigs.

SILVER BUFFALOBERRY *Shepherdia argentea* Nutt.
A shrub or small tree with foliage, twigs, and buds *silver-scaly.* Leaves *1"- 2 1/2"* long, ± leathery, bases *V-shaped.* Twigs often *thorn-tipped*; bud scales *two*; bundle scar *one.* Flowers small, green, without petals, April-June; fruits small, orange-red, fleshy, July-September. To 15' in height. Ranging west across the plains to sw. Alberta /w. Montana /Wyoming, locally to w. Nevada, sw. Utah, and cen. New Mexico. Fruits said to be useful for jelly. Russian-olive (Plate 33), a widely-planted and sometimes thorny imported tree, also has silvery foliage but the leaves are alternate.

RED-OSIER DOGWOOD *Cornus sericea* L.
Like all dogwoods, this continent-wide and mostly-shrubby species has oval leaves whose lateral veins tend to *follow the leaf edges.* Leaves 2"- 4" long, ± hairy, with *4-7* pairs of side veins. Twigs *bright red,* twig leaf scars *raised,* buds *2-scaled,* bundle scars *three,* and pith *white.* Flowers small, white, in flat-topped clusters, May-July; fruits small, *white,* fleshy, July-December. To 26' tall. Moist sites. Also called American Dogwood; formerly *C. stolonifera* Michx. Twigs browsed by deer and rabbits.

BUTTONBUSH *Cephalanthus occidentalis* L.
A widespread shrub or small tree of wet soils and usually with some leaves in *whorls* of three or four. Buds ± scaly and mostly *buried* in the bark. Bundle scar *single.* Pith *brown.* Flowers small, white, in tight *balls* at twig ends. Fruits *dry,* long-stemmed, in *spherical* heads 3/4"- 1" wide. Height sometimes to 20'-30'. Transcontinental; in the Southwest mainly Arizona.

DESERT-OLIVE FORESTIERA *Forestiera pubescens* Nutt.
A small *near-evergreen* tree of s. Arizona with leaves 1"- 1 1/2" long, *1/8"- 1/4"* wide, *blunt, wedge-based,* and edges *rolled under.* Leaves may be clustered on *spur branches.* Bundle scar *one.* Fruits small, black, single-seeded, with a thin fleshy covering. Charles LaForestier was a French naturalist of the 1800s. Formerly *F. phillyreoides* (Benth.) Torr.

Plate 12

SILVER
BUFFALOBERRY

SINGLELEAF
ASH

RED-OSIER
DOGWOOD

BUTTONBUSH

DESERT-OLIVE
FORESTIERA

IV. Trees with Alternate Compound Leaves
Plates 13-20

The trees of Plates 13-20 have alternate *feather-compound* foliage (trees with fan-compound leaves grow wild in other regions). Thorny trees are on Plates 13-15. *Do not mistake the leaflets of a compound leaf for the blades of simple leaves* (see Fig. 1, page 8).

13. TREES THORNY, LEAVES ONCE-COMPOUND

These trees are legumes, all with *pealike* blossoms and *pod* fruits.

NEW MEXICO LOCUST *Robinia neomexicana* A. Gray

A small tree, the leaves *4"- 10"* long with 9-21 smooth-edged, *bristle-tipped* leaflets. Leaflets 3/4"- 1 1/2" long and 1/2"- 1" wide. Twigs hairy or not, thorns *paired*, 1/4"- 1/2" long, flanking the leaf scars. Buds *break through* the leaf scars in spring. Bundle scars 3. Spur branches *lacking*. Flowers *pink-purple* in drooping clusters *2"- 4"* long, spring; fruit pods 2"- 6" in length, *brown-hairy*, autumn or later. Height to 25'. Mountains, se. Nevada and cen. Colorado to w. Texas and n. Mexico. Deer browse the twigs; wild turkeys and other birds eat the seeds. Native Americans ate the fresh flowers and cooked the seeds.

BLACK LOCUST *Robinia pseudoacacia* L.

Like New Mexico Locust but with leaves *8"- 14"* long, the leaflets *smoothly blunt-tipped* and occasionally fine-toothed. Height 70'- 100'. Native in the East but spreading rapidly; it may occur anywhere in our area. Makes durable fence posts. Seeds and bark listed as poisonous to livestock and people.

DESERT IRONWOOD *Olneya tesota* A. Gray

This tree usually presents a dense mass of thick, gray-green, *evergreen* leaves each *2"- 4"* long and with 8-20 blunt, fine-hairy leaflets each *1/2"- 3/4"* in length. Twigs greenish and hairless, often with thorns *both* paired and single, sometimes with small spur branches. Flowers lavendar, each 1/2" long, in clusters to 1 1/2" in length, May-June. Fruit pods 1"-3" long, hairy, and narrowed between the 1-6 black seeds. Trunk bark gray-shreddy. Height 25'-30'. Desert washes and depressions, se. California /sw. Arizona. One of the heaviest American woods; fresh wood will not float. Outstanding for firewood and becoming scarce. Native Americans made arrowheads of the wood, ate the flowers, and made flour of the seeds. Intolerant of cold. Also called Tesota (teh-SO-tah) and Palo de Hierro (PAH-lo-day-YAIR-oh), Spanish for Ironwood.

SOUTHWESTERN CORALBEAN *Erythrina flabelliformis* Kearn.

Usually *leafless* but with bright red springtime flowers. Leaves 5"-12" long with 3 wide, triangular, toothless leaflets, each 2"- 4" long. Twigs stout, often *white-hairy,* with small, *single* thorns 1/8"- 1/4" in length. Fruits 4"- 10" long, seeds *scarlet.* To 15' tall. Se.Arizona and sw. New Mexico south to w. Mexico.

Plate 13

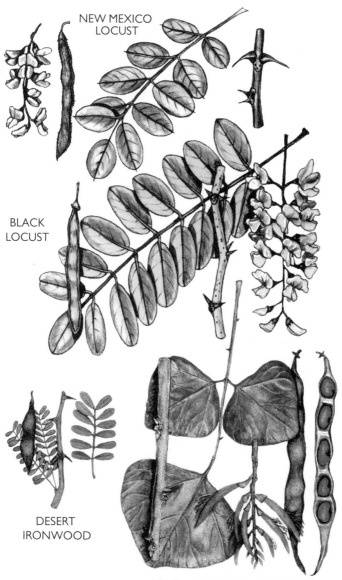

NEW MEXICO LOCUST

BLACK LOCUST

DESERT IRONWOOD

SOUTHWESTERN CORALBEAN

14.THORNS PAIRED, LEAVES TWICE-COMPOUND

These are leguminous plants of arid or semi-arid soils with leaves divided into *major* leaflets and again into *minor* leaflets (see Figure 1, page 8). Thorns are *straight* or slightly curved. These species have thorns mostly *paired,* spur branches *present*, leaflets *blunt* and *smooth-edged,* flowers *pealike*, and *pod* fruits. Mesquites have only *one pair* of major leaflets (rarely 2-3 pairs). See footnote, Plate 20.

HONEY MESQUITE *Prosopis glandulosa* Torr.
A small tree or shrub with leaves *5"- 10"* long. Each of the two major leaflets has 10-20 pairs of *hairless* minor leaflets *3/4"- 1 1/2"* in length and *1/8"- 1/4"* wide. Spur branches ± *3/8"* long are *prominent* on the branchlets. Thorns, often single, are *± 1"* in length. Flowers white to *pale yellow,* in slender clusters, *2"- 7"* long, April-July; fruit pods cylindrical, brown, *4"- 10"* long, and *± beaded.* Trunk dark, often *nearly black.* Height to 20'. Rangelands, se. California, sw. Utah, and n. Texas to s. Mexico. Once confined to streamsides by grassland wildfires but heavy grazing and fire control have enabled its spread into uplands. Useful for fence posts, firewood, and charcoal. Cattle, deer, and other species browse the twigs and eat the pods. A good honey plant. Native Americans made cakes and a fermented drink using flour made from the seeds. Pronounced mes-keetay in Spanish.

VELVET MESQUITE *Prosopis velutina* Woot.
Much like Honey Mesquite but with 15-20 pairs of *± hairy* minor leaflets each only *1/4" -1/2"* long and *1/16"- 1/8"* wide. Thorns often few. Spur branches *short.* Height to 50'. From cen. Arizona and sw. New Mexico south into Mexico.

SCREWBEAN MESQUITE *Prosopis pubescens* Benth.
A mesquite with *tightly-spiralled* fruit pods *1"- 3"* long. Leaves only *1"- 3"* in length with *5-9* pairs of minor leaflets *1/4"- 3/8"* long and *1/8"- 3/16"* wide. Seeds eaten by bobwhites, Gambel quail, roadrunners, and other wildlife. S. California, s. Nevada, and sw. Arizona to nw. Mexico. Also, the Rio Grande valley.

HUISACHE *Acacia farnesiana* (L.) Willd.
A shrub or small tree of Mexico and border areas. Leaves have *4-8 pairs of major leaflets* each with 10-25 pairs of minor leaflets *1/4" long and 1/32"* wide. Flower clusters yellow, ball-shaped, fragrant. Pronounced wee-SAH-chay; also called Sweet Acacia.

JERUSALEM-THORN *Parkinsonia aculeata* L.
After 40-60 tiny minor leaflets drop early, *2-6 grasslike midribs* each 8"- 15" long remain as remnants of the major leaflets. Thorns are often triple with one longer. Spur branches small. Flowers yellow. Bark *green.* To 35' tall. Also called Mexican Paloverde or Retama (reh-TAH-mah). John Parkinson was an English botanist of the 16th century. South from s. Arizona and s. Texas.

Plate 14

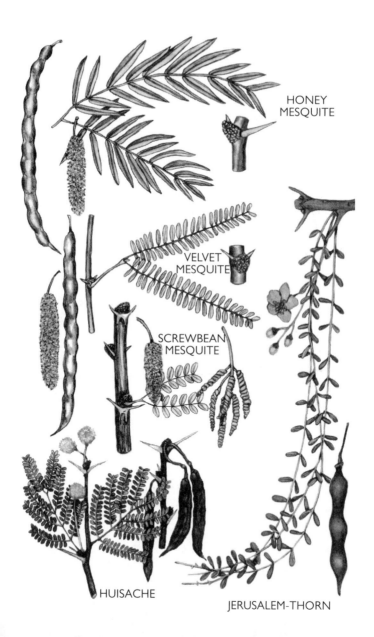

HONEY MESQUITE

VELVET MESQUITE

SCREWBEAN MESQUITE

HUISACHE

JERUSALEM-THORN

15. THORNS SINGLE, LEAVES TWICE-COMPOUND

Trees with foliage divided into *major* leaflets and again into *minor* leaflets, the latter *blunt* and *not* toothed. Leguminous trees with flowers *pealike*; fruits in *pods*. Catclaw acacias have thorns mostly *single, curved, hooklike,* and 1/4"- 3/8" long. Arid /semi-arid sites.

BLUE PALOVERDE *Cercidium floridum* A. Gray

A desert tree with leaves only *3/4"- 1"* long, *mostly absent.* The ephemeral foliage has *one* pair of major leaflets, each with *1-3* pairs of minor leaflets only 3/16"- 1/4" long and ± *1/16"* wide. Unlike Yellow Paloverde (Plate 21), a thorn 1/4"- 3/8" in length occurs *at each node.* Thorns *straight.* Flowers showy, *yellow,* about 3/4" wide, in loose clusters, March-May; fruit pods *flat,* 2"- 3" long. Trunk and large branches mostly *smooth* and *blue-green.* Height to 30'. Young pods and seeds were foods of Native Americans. Desert washes and depressions south from se. California and sw. Arizona. Pronounced pah-low-VEHR-deh.

GREGG CATCLAW *Acacia greggii* A. Gray

Leaves are *1"-3"* long with *1-3* pairs of major leaflets and *3-7* pairs of minor leaflets each *1/8"- 1/4"* long and *1/16"* wide. Spur branches about 1/4" long. Flowers *pale yellow,* in *slender* clusters, 2"- 3" long, fragrant; fruit pods *much twisted,* brown, hairless. Trunk bark gray-brown, deeply fissured. Height 15'- 30'. From se. California, s. Nevada, and sw. Utah, across cen. and s. Arizona to w. Texas and nearby Mexico. Thicket-forming, drought-resistant; browsed by deer and livestock despite the thorns. A fine honey plant. Native Americans once ate the fruit pods raw or cooked and ground the seeds into flour.

In w. Texas and adjoining Mexico there are three additional catclaws: **Roemer Catclaw** (*A. roemeriana* Scheele), also found in se. New Mexico, has leaves *1 1/2"- 4"* in length with *1-3* pairs of major leaflets and *3-8* pairs of minor leaflets each of which is *1/4"- 1/2"* long and *1/8"- 1/4"* wide. Some thorns may be paired. Flower clusters yellowish, *globular.* **Wright Catclaw** (*A. wrightii* Benth.) is similar but leaves are *1"-3"* long with only *1-2* major leaflet pairs and flowers in slim *spikes.* **Guajillo** (*A. berlandieri* Benth.), occasionally with thorns absent or not curved, has *large fernlike* leaves with *5-12* pairs of major leaflets and numerous minor leaflets *1/8"- 3/16"* long and ± *1/32"* wide. Near the Mexican border, the *straight-thorned* **Dwarf Poinciana** [*Caesalpinia pulcherrima* (L.) Sw.] also may escape from plantings. Leaves *nearly evergreen,* *5"- 15"* long with *5-10* major and *6-10* minor leaflet pairs. Minor leaflets *3/8"- 3/4"* long and ± *5/16"* wide. Flowers large, *showy,* petals red and yellow, stamens long, red. "Dwarf" compared with Royal Poinciana or Flamboyant [*Delonix regia* (Bojer ex Hook.) Raf.], a related flowering tree widely planted in the tropics.

Plate 15

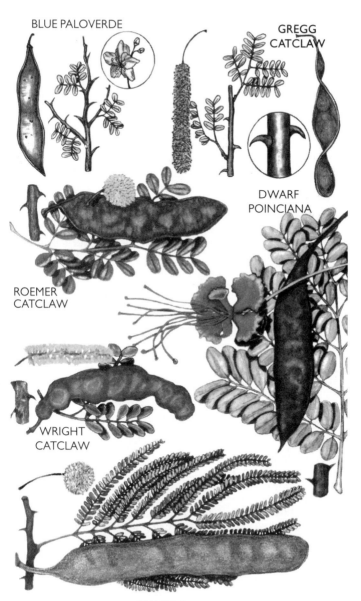

BLUE PALOVERDE

GREGG
CATCLAW

DWARF
POINCIANA

ROEMER
CATCLAW

WRIGHT
CATCLAW

GUAJILLO

16. LEAVES ONCE-COMPOUND and TOOTHED

There are only a few *non-thorny deciduous* trees in our area with leaves *once-compound* and *toothed*. Their leaves are *5"- 24"* long with *5-41* leaflets, bundle scars are *many,* and spur branches are *lacking.* **Walnuts** have leaves *spicy-scented* when crushed, twigs *stout,* leaf scars *large* and *shield-shaped or triangular,* and pith *chambered.* Male blossoms in slender catkins, spring; female flowers tiny. Fruits nearly *spherical.* nuts, edible; fruit husks stain hands and clothes brown (be careful!). Lumber valuable for furniture. Bruised branches and foliage will stun fish, a practice illegal in the United States. English Walnut (*J. regia* L.), sometimes planted, has leaves *not* toothed. **Smooth Sumac and Mexican-buckeye** have leaf scars *C-shaped or lobed,* and pith *solid.* On Plate 17, Common Hoptree sometimes has leaves ± fine-toothed while Prairie Sumac and Tree-of-Heaven may be few-toothed.

ARIZONA WALNUT *Juglans major* (Torr.) A. Heller
Leaves 9"- 13" long with *9-15* leaflets each 2"- 4" in length, *3/4"- 1 1/4"* wide, long-pointed, *coarse-toothed,* and sometimes curved. Fruits *1"- 1 1/2"* in diameter. Height 30'- 50'. At 2000'- 7500' elevations from cen. Arizona, w-cen. New Mexico, and cen. Texas south to Mexico.

TEXAS WALNUT *Juglans microcarpa* Berlandier
A small-fruited walnut with leaves 8"- 16" long and leaflets *15-21 (25)* in number, 2"- 6" long, only *1/4"- 1/2"* wide, long-pointed, frequently curved, and with or without *fine* teeth. Fruits *3/4"- 1"* in diameter. Height to 20'. Streamsides, sw. Kansas and nw. New Mexico to Mexico.

SMOOTH SUMAC *Rhus glabra* L.
A small tree of the East, local in the Southwest. Leaves with *11-31* long-pointed, *coarse-toothed* leaflets. Twigs *stout, flat-sided;* leaf scars *C-shaped,* and buds *white-hairy.* Flowers small, *greenish,* June-July; fruits tiny, dry, *red-hairy* clusters, July-winter. Height 4'- 10' (25'). Native Americans reportedly ate the raw sprouts.

MEXICAN-BUCKEYE *Ungnadia speciosa* Endl.
This small tree or shrub has *5-7 coarse-toothed,* long-pointed leaflets, attractive springtime blossoms, and curious fruits. Leaf scars and fruits *3-lobed;* the latter *pear-shaped.* Twigs *slender,* short-hairy; buds dark, blunt. Flowers *pink,* ± 1" wide. Seeds shiny, dark, about 1/2" in diameter, reportedly *poisonous.* Height to 30'. Often *several-stemmed* and good for landscaping. Limestone soils, from se. New Mexico and cen. Texas to n. Mexico. Baron von Ungnad was an Austrian diplomat. Called Monilla (mo-NEE-yah) in Mexico.

Plate 16

ARIZONA
WALNUT

TEXAS
WALNUT

SMOOTH
SUMAC

MEXICAN-
BUCKEYE

17. LEAVES ONCE-COMPOUND, NOT TOOTHED I

These are *deciduous* trees with leaves 4"- 24" long and leaflets 1/4"- 2" wide. Tree-of-Heaven leaflets may *appear* to be without teeth but there are 2-4 small gland-teeth at the leaflet bases. See also English and Texas walnuts (Plate 16).

COMMON HOPTREE *Ptelea trifoliata* L.
Our only tree regularly with *alternate trifoliate* foliage. Leaves 4"- 10" long; each leaflet 1"- 4" long and 1/2"- 2" wide, gland-dotted (use lens), and occasionally fine-toothed. End leaflet *short-stalked* and twigs hairless. Hairy buds *hidden* beneath leafstalk bases or nearly surrounded by *U-shaped* leaf scars. Bundle scars three. Small, green, spring flowers produce *flat,* circular, *papery,* hoplike fruits 3/4"-1" across. Trunk bark pale and smooth or shallowly grooved. Height to 15'. From s. Nevada, sw. Utah, and cen. Colorado to the East Coast.

WESTERN SOAPBERRY *Sapindus drummondii* Hook. & Arn.
A tree whose 4"- 15" leaves have *8-18 narrow, long-pointed,* and somewhat-leathery leaflets. Leaflets each 1"- 3" long and 3/4"- 1" wide with the sides *unequal.* End leaflet often *lacking* but may be the only leaflet retained in winter. Buds small, hairy, and *partially imbedded* (use lens). Leaf scars triangular or 3-lobed, *not* surrounding the buds. Bundle scars three, often obscure. Flowers white, clustered, June-July; fruits *spherical, fleshy,* yellowish to white, 3/8"- 1/2" in diameter, September-October. Height 20'- 50' (70'). Arizona /New Mexico, east to the Mississippi Valley, and south to Mexico. Named *S. saponaria* var. *drummondii* (Hook. & Arn.) L. Benson by some botanists.

PRAIRIE SUMAC *Rhus lanceolata* (Gray) Britton
Local in se. New Mexico and w. Texas. The 5"- 10" leaves with *11-23 narrow, long-pointed* leaflets 1/4"- 1/2" wide are sometimes few-toothed. Midrib *winged* (use lens). Twigs stout, hairless; pith large. Buds *partly surrounded* by leafstalk bases or leaf scars. Bundle scars many. Fruits small, *red-hairy.* Bark has been used to tan leather.

TREE-OF-HEAVEN *Ailanthus altissima* (Mill.) Swingle
Chinese in origin and fast-growing, but generally of little value. Leaves *12"- 24"* long with *11-41* leaflets each 2"- 6" in length and 3/4"- 2" wide. Leaflets have *only 1-2 pairs of gland-teeth* near the base. Twigs thick but weak, pith *continuous*; buds small, hairy. Bundle scars many. Flowers small, yellow, early summer; fruits one-seeded, papery, in large clusters, autumn. To 100' tall on disturbed sites throughout the United States. May grow 8' or more a year; sprouts 12' long are not unusual. The common name, probably of Asiatic origin, may allude to the tree's height.

Plate 17

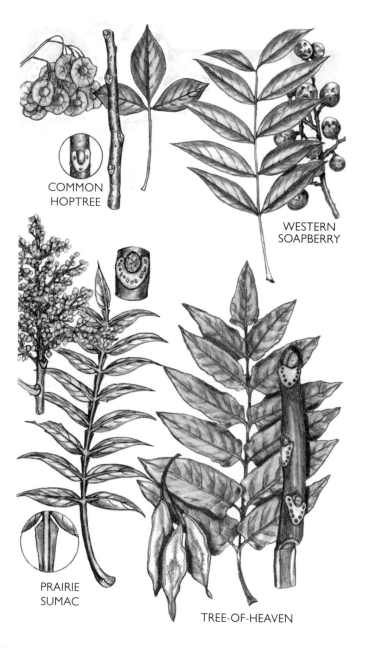

COMMON
HOPTREE

WESTERN
SOAPBERRY

PRAIRIE
SUMAC

TREE-OF-HEAVEN

18. LEAVES ONCE-COMPOUND, NOT TOOTHED II

These are arid-zone shrubs or small trees with foliage *much reduced in size* (leaflets mostly less than 1/8" wide) and *deciduous* during dry periods. Compare Plate 17.

WESTERN KIDNEYWOOD *Eysenhardtia polystachya* (Ort.) Sarg.
A small tree or shrub whose leaves are *1"- 4"* long with *20-56 narrow, blunt* leaflets each only *1/4"- 1/2"* long and *1/16"- 1/8"* wide. The foliage yields a *resinous* odor and displays dark *gland dots* (use lens). Twigs gray-brown, slender, *flexible.* Flowers white, in 2"- 3" spikes; fruit pods flat, and only 1/4"- 1/2" long. Trunk bark gray, *peeling.* Se. Arizona and sw. New Mexico to n. Mexico; also cen. Mexico. Browsed by livestock and deer. A good honey plant. Wood yields an orange dye reportledly used in some areas for kidney and bladder illnesses.

ELEPHANT-TREE *Bursera microphylla* Gray.
An uncommon tree in the hottest and driest rocky deserts in se. California, s. Arizona, and nw. Mexico. Leaves only *1"- 1 1/2"* long, divided into *20-40* tiny leaflets, and with a *spicy* odor when crushed. Midribs *winged* (use lens). Twigs *red-brown, stubby,* and often crowded with leaf scars and buds. The tree has a short, stout, *tapering* trunk with *thin* bark that *peels* in several layers. Sap *red.* Related to frankincense and myrrh of the Bible; the aromatic resin is said to be burned in some churches and in Native American ceremonies. The gum is said to be useful to treat scorpion stings. Both the tree and its' resin are known as Copal in some districts. Height 5'- 25'. Sunny sites.

FRAGRANT BURSERA *Bursera fagaroides* (H.B.K.) Engler
Though thus far reported in the United States only near Fresnal, Pima County, Arizona, this tree is more widely distributed in Sonora, Baja California, and cen. Mexico. The aromatic leaves are *1"- 2"* long with *5-11* leaflets often *pointed.* Twigs stubby; spur branches common. Trunk bark *peeling.* To 15' tall.

LITTLELEAF SUMAC *Rhus microphylla* Engelm.
Leaves only *1"- 1 1/2"* long with *5-9* stalkless and ± long-hairy leaflets each about 3/8" long and 1/8" wide. Leafstalks *winged.* Twigs short, stiff, and somewhat *spiky.* Fruits clustered and *red-hairy.* Height to 15'. A relative of Evergreen Sumac (Plate 19) found from se. Arizona and cen. Texas south to cen. Mexico. Also local in sw. Okla., nw. Texas, and ne. New Mexico.

Plate 18

WESTERN
KIDNEYWOOD

ELEPHANT-TREE

GLAND
DOTS

FRAGRANT
BURSERA

LITTLELEAF
SUMAC

WINGED
LEAFSTALKS

19. LEAVES ONCE-COMPOUND and EVERGREEN

Trees with shiny, leathery leaflets that lack teeth:

EVERGREEN SUMAC *Rhus choriophylla* Woots. & Standl.
A small tree or shrub with leaves *2"- 3"* long and the *3-5* (-7) leaflets *1"- 2"* long, 1/2"- 7/8" wide, *pointed*, and hairless. End leaflet *long-stalked.* Twigs *hairless.* Flowers greenish, July-Aug.; fruits *red-hairy,* in dense clusters. Along the international border from se. Arizona to w. Texas. Also known as Mearns Sumac.

MESCALBEAN SOPHORA *Sophora secundiflora* (Ort.) Lag. ex DC
Found from s-cen. New Mexico and cen. Texas to s. Mexico, this species has leaves *4"- 6"* long with *5-9 blunt-tipped* leaflets each 3/4"- 2" long, 1/2"- 1" wide, the midribs grooved. Twigs greenish, often *hairy.* Flowers pealike, showy, purple, fragrant, March-April; fruit pods stout, somewhat beaded, 1"- 5" long; seeds large, red, and poisonous! Often called Coralbean but not to be confused with the thorny Southwestern Coralbean of Plate 13.

BRAZILIAN PEPPERTREE *Schinus terebinthifolius* Raddi
A tropical tree planted widely in warm areas. Leaves *3"- 6"* long with *3–11* leaflets each *1 1/2"– 3"* long and *3/4"– 1"* wide. Leaflets rounded or short-pointed at the tip, wedge-based, sometimes wavy-toothed, *increasing* in width toward the tip and with a turpentine odor when crushed. Midrib *red* and narrowly winged. Twigs hairless, *not* drooping. Flower small, yellow-white, in clusters at the leaf angles, summer. Fruits 1/8"–3/16" in diameter, red, 1-seeded, autumn–winter. Height to 20'. Occurs in s. California, s. Arizona, and perhaps elsewhere. Becoming a pest in s. Florida, displacing native species. Popular for Christmas decoration.

PERU PEPPERTREE *Schinus molle* L.
Leaflets more *narrow,* numerous, and *long-pointed* than in Brazilian Peppertree Leaves *6"–10"* long with *17–41* short- or long-pointed leaflets each *1"– 2"* long, *1/8"– 1/4"* wide and sometimes fine-toothed. Twigs *droop.* Flowers tiny, in prominent 5"– 12" branched sprays. Fruits reddish, 1/8"– 1/4"in diameter, 1-seeded, aromatic, in large clusters. Height to 50 ft. Planted from California to Texas and may spread on its own. Seeds reported sometimes to be crushed and used to adulterate or substitute for the (East Asian) black pepper (*Piper nigrum* L.) of commerce.

Plate 19

EVERGREEN
SUMAC

MESCALBEAN

BRAZILIAN
PEPPERTREE

PERU
PEPPERTREE

20. LEAVES TWICE-COMPOUND

Most Southwestern trees with twice-compound leaves are thorny (see Plates 14-15). Only the following few non-thorny leguminous* trees also have foliage of this type. They are mainly *evergreen*, with bundle scars *three* or obscure, and fruit pods *flat*. Guajillo (Plate 15) sometimes also may be thornless.

LITTLELEAF LYSILOMA *Lysiloma microphylla* Benth.

A mostly Mexican species that extends northward only to the Rinçon Mts. of se. Ariz. Leaves 2"– 5" long with *4–9* pairs of major leaflets and *25–35* pairs of minor leaflets. Each of the latter 3/16" long and up to *1/16"* wide. Flowers in *globular* heads, *white*. Fruit pods *4"– 8"* in length. Rocky slopes, 3000'– 4000' elevations. Rarely tree size in the United States probably because of colder winters. Also called Feather-tree or Desert-fern.

PARADISE POINCIANA *Caesalpinia gilliesii* (Hook.) Dietr.

A shrub or tree of Argentina that is becoming established from s. California to cen. Texas. Leaves 4"– 12" long with *6–12* pairs of major leaflets, each of which has *5–10* pairs of minor leaflets. Minor leaflets about *3/16"* long and *1/16" –1/8"* wide. Flowers *showy, yellow with long red stamens;* 3/4"– 1 1/2" in diameter, in *loose clusters* at twig ends, summer. Fruit pods *2"– 4"* long, *velvety*. Height to 15 ft. Dry soils. Also w-cen. Mexico. Odor offensive to some people. Also known as Bird-of-Paradise (but not the florists' Bird-of-Paradise, *Strelitzia reginae* Banks, a nonwoody South African species). The genus was named after Andreas Caesalpinus, an Italian physician, while the species name honors John Gillies, an 18th-century botanist who discovered the plant.

GOLDENBALL LEADTREE *Leucaena retusa* Benth.

A shrub or small tree whose leaves are 3"- 8" long with only 2–4 (*mostly 3*) pairs of major leaflets. Minor leaflets 3–9 (*usually 3–6)* pairs per major leaflet, each minor leaflet *1/2"– 7/8"* long, *3/8"– 1/2"* wide, and mostly with tiny points on the otherwise rounded foliage (use lens). Some leaflets, however, are notched at the end rather than with extended tips. Leaf scars are ± circular; bud scales have long points. Flowers in *yellow balls* 3/4" wide, April–Oct. Fruit pods dark, *6"– 10"* long. Height to 25', but rarely a tree in the United States. Mountain canyons in w. Texas and n. Mexico; also in western parts of the Edwards Plateau, cen. Texas. Also called Littleleaf Leadtree or Wahoo-tree.

---

*Space was not available earlier (Plates 13-15) but it should be noted that most legumes (members of pea-bean families) grow root nodules containing bacteria that convert atmospheric nitrogen into soil-enriching compounds. This benefits both legumes and neighboring plants.

Plate 20

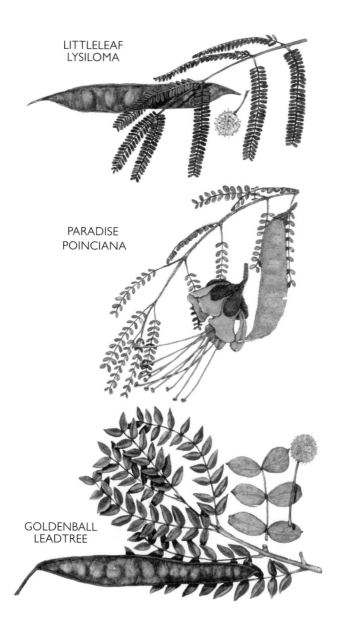

LITTLELEAF
LYSILOMA

PARADISE
POINCIANA

GOLDENBALL
LEADTREE

V. Trees with Alternate Simple Leaves
Plates 21-39

Thin *deciduous* leaves occur in 57 of our species while 18 kinds have mostly-leathery *evergreen* foliage. But see Yellow Paloverde below.

21. LEAFLESS DESERT TREES, TWIGS SPINE-TIPPED

Leaves are *much reduced in size* (to 1/4"- 1") and *present only for a short time* in spring. The *mostly-greenish* twigs and branches function as foliage in the photosynthetic process. Flowers are in lateral clusters. The first three species are all sometimes called Crucifixion-thorn. Only Canotia reaches north to s. Utah. Desert Apricot and Bitter Condalia (Plate 22) also are often leafless.

ALLTHORN *Koeberlinia spinosa* Zucc.
An extremely-thorny species with *stout,* yellow- or blue-green twigs 1"- 2" long, mostly at *right angles* to the branchlets, and with short, *black* spiny ends. Flowers greenish, in small clusters, March-July; fruits shiny, *black berries* 1/4" wide. Ranges from se. California, cen. Arizona, cen. New Mexico, and s. Texas to cen. Mexico. Jackrabbits browse the twigs; scaled quail eat the fruits. C. L. Koeberlin was a 19th century German botanist.

CRUCIFIXION-THORN *Castela emoryi* (Gray) Moran & Felger
This small tree has stiff, *stout,* yellow-green twigs mostly 3"- 5" long and ± fine-hairy (use lens). The tiny leaf scars are *greenish-white* (use lens). Flowers purplish, about 1/4" across, densely clustered, June-July. Brown, dry, 1-seeded fruits *persist* on the tree *in starlike rings.* Height to 15'. Desert washes, se. California and sw. Arizona to nw. Mexico. Lt. Col. William Emory directed the Mexican boundary survey. Formerly *Holacantha.*

CANOTIA *Canotia holacantha* Torr.
The *slim,* yellow-green, fine-grooved (use lens) twigs of this species show tiny *black,* ± triangular, leaf scars (use lens). Flowers greenish, in small groups, May-August; fruits dry, persistent, 5- (10-) parted capsules, 1/2" long. Older trunk bark *dark.* To 20' tall. Deserts, s. Utah and Arizona to nw. Mexico.

SMOKETHORN *Psorothamnus spinosa* (A. Gray) Barnaby
Gray-green, white-hairy, and *slender* twigs give a *smoky* tinge to this plant. Leaf scars are brownish (use lens). Flowers purple, June; fruits tiny, 1-seeded pea pods. Trunk *gray.* Height to 25'. Se. California, s. Nevada, and sw. Arizona. Formerly *Dalea.*

YELLOW PALOVERDE *Cercidium microphyllum* (Torr.) Rose & Johnst.
(Foliage twice-compound but usually leafless, therefor reviewed here.) Common along desert washes of se. California, s. Arizona, and nw. Mexico, usually with a smooth *yellow-green* trunk and branches. Springtime leaves are 3/4"- 1" long with two major leaflets each with 4-8 pairs of minor leaflets. The *slender* twigs have small *dark* leaf scars. Compare Blue Paloverde, Plate 15.

Plate 21

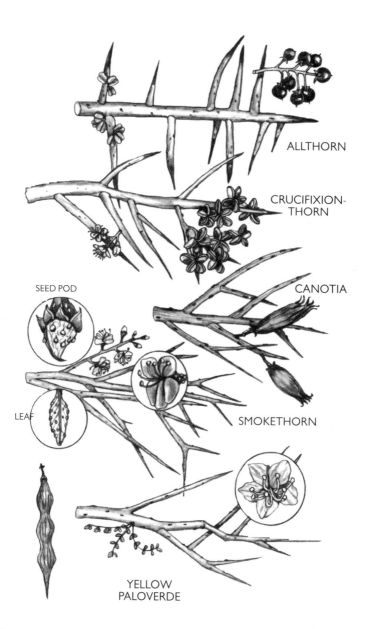

ALLTHORN

CRUCIFIXION-
THORN

CANOTIA

SEED POD

LEAF

SMOKETHORN

YELLOW
PALOVERDE

22. THORNY TREES with LEAVES NORMAL

Only these few trees have alternate simple foliage and regularly produce thorns or sharp-tipped spur branches. They mostly have three bundle scars and white springtime flowers. All except the last two have leaves toothed; Hollyleaf Buckthorn is evergreen. Russian-olive (Plate 33) also sometimes bears thorns.

Hawthorns are shrubs or small trees with dense foliage. Thorns are *slender,* 1"- 2" long, occurring on *both* twigs and older wood, and mostly do *not* bear buds or leaves. Leaf bases *V-shaped;* spur branches mostly *absent.* Fruits small, applelike, mostly *several-seeded,* summer-winter. Though easily identified as a group, even experts have difficulty recognizing species. Black Hawthorn is the most common in the West and serves here as an example. Often used by songbirds as nest sites. Invades pastures. Also called Thornapple.

BLACK HAWTHORN *Crataegus douglasii* Lindl.
Foliage 1"- 4" long, *coarsely double-toothed* or shallow-lobed, mostly *hairless.* Thorns *1/3"- 1"* long. Mature fruits *black.* To 25' tall. From cen. British Columbia to cen. Arizona /New Mexico.

AMERICAN PLUM *Prunus americana* Marsh.
A small tree or shrub of the northern plains ranging eastward from w. Montana, cen. Colorado, and cen. New Mexico. Leaves 1"- 5" long, about half as wide, ± long-pointed, sharply and mostly *double-toothed.* Leafstalk glands *lacking.* Thorns are mostly short, stiff, bud-bearing spur branches; twigs sometimes hairy. Fruits red or yellow, 3/4"- 1" in diameter, *single-seeded.* Height 15'- 30'. Thicket-forming. Fruits much eaten by wildlife.

DESERT APRICOT *Prunus fremontii* Wats.
A shrub or small tree with leaves ± *circular,* mostly *under 1"* long, fine-toothed, hairless, and veins reddish. Twigs short, stiff. Trunk red-brown to gray. Flowers February-March. Fruits about 1/2" wide, yellowish, fine-hairy, with only a thin layer of edible flesh. Deserts of se. California and Baja California.

HOLLYLEAF BUCKTHORN *Rhamnus ilicifolia* Kellogg
An *evergreen* shrub or small tree with *thorn-tipped* twigs and *prickly-edged* leaves only 1/4"- 1" long, leathery, with parallel veins. Flowers yellowish, April-May; fruits red, with *1-3* seeds, June-July. To 25' tall. Found over much of California /Arizona.

BITTER CONDALIA *Condalia globosa* I. M. Johnst.
This *extremely-spiny* tree has *smooth-edged,* blunt, wedge-based leaves only 1/4"- 1/2" long. *Spine-tipped* twigs form *right angles* with each other. Bundle scar *one.* Fruits black, fleshy, bitter. Desert mountains, se. California, sw. Arizona, and nw. Mexico.

CHITTAMWOOD *Sideroxylon lanuginosa* Michx.
A shrubby tree with leaves blunt, V-based, ± leathery, and 1"- 4" long. Sap *milky.* South from se. Arizona /sw. New Mexico. Formerly *Bumelia lanuginosa* (Michx.) Pers., Gum Bumelia.

Plate 22

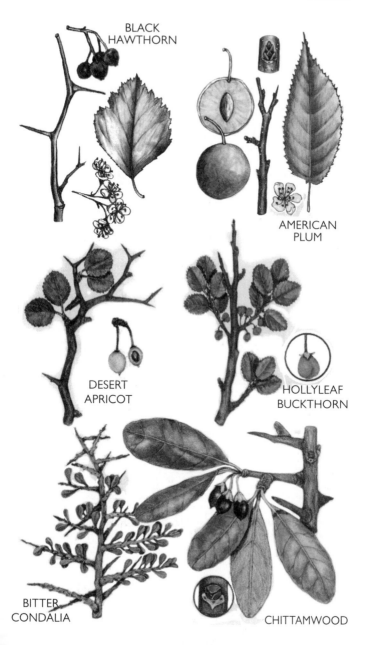

BLACK HAWTHORN

AMERICAN PLUM

DESERT APRICOT

HOLLYLEAF BUCKTHORN

BITTER CONDALIA

CHITTAMWOOD

23. THORNLESS TREES: LEAVES FAN-LOBED

Alternate fan-lobed leaves occur in few trees of the Southwest .
Among these, the last three species may have foliage both fan-lobed
and fan-veined (see also White Poplar, Plate 25). Hawthorns
(Plate 22) also may have alternate fan-lobed leaves but the plants are
thorny. Most maples (Plate 11) have *opposite* fan-lobed foliage.

ARIZONA SYCAMORE *Platanus wrightii* S.Wats.

Sycamores typically are floodplain trees with *mottled* and *flaky*
outer brown bark exposing a *pale* underbark, but in this species
the trunk and main branches may be nearly white. Leaves deeply
5-7 lobed, 4"- 10" long, and *without* teeth. Leafstalk with a *hollow*
base that covers the bud. A leaf scar with *many* bundle scars
surrounds each bud. Bud with a *single* caplike scale. A leafy
stipule *encircles* the twig near each bud, leaving a stipule scar that
rings the winter twig. Springtime heads of small, fuzzy, greenish
flowers produce tiny, hairy, brown fruits in tight inch-wide *balls;*
3-5 balls hang on each stalk. Height to 80'. From cen. Arizona and
sw. New Mexico southward. Willows (Plates 30-32), also have a
single bud scale but otherwise are different.

CALIFORNIA FREMONTIA
Fremontodendron californicum (Torr.) Cov.

A brightly-flowered plant with *evergreen* fan-lobed foliage.
Leaves leathery, mostly only *1"- 2"* long, rather *sandpapery*
above, *densely hairy* beneath, and long-stalked. Usually 3-5 lobes
per leaf with 1-3 main veins meeting at the leafbase. Some leaves
wavy-toothed, others smooth-edged. Twigs and buds *brown-
hairy;* buds *without* scales; bundle scar *single;* spur branches
present. Blossoms *yellow,* 1"- 2 1/2"across, May-June; fruit
capsules hairy, egg-shaped, 1"- 1 1/4" long, August-September.
Often shrubby but sometimes to 25' tall. California, Baja
California, and across cen. Arizona. Named after
John C. Frémont, 19th century frontiersman and politician.

TEXAS MULBERRY *Morus microphylla* Buckl.

A mulberry with leaves *deciduous*, toothed, *rough-hairy* on both
sides, often many-lobed, and only *1"- 3"* long. Bud scales 3-5,
bundle scars *4 or more*, and sap *milky* in warm weather. Fruits
dark, blackberrylike, edible, May-June. Height to 20'. From
cen. and s. Arizona to s. Oklahoma and n. Mexico. Inner bark
fibrous, can be twisted into cords and pounded into bark cloth.

WHITE MULBERRY *Morus alba* L.

Like the last species but leaves *3"– 10"* long, mostly 3–5-lobed,
hairless. Bud scales 5-6. Fruits *whitish,* ± tasteless. Introduced
from China in 1600s to raise silkworms. Widely naturalized.

Plate 23

ARIZONA SYCAMORE

CALIFORNIA FREMONTIA

TEXAS MULBERRY

WHITE MULBERRY

24. LEAVES FAN-VEINED OR HEART-SHAPED

Unlobed foliage that regularly has three or more main veins meeting at the leaf base marks these trees. Some plants of Plate 23 and some poplars (Plate 25) have similar leaf venation. Bundle scars are *three*.

NETLEAF HACKBERRY *Celtis reticulata* Torr.
A tree with trunk otherwise rather dark and smooth but marked by prominent *warty knobs*. Foliage *sandpaper-textured* above, *net-veined* beneath, and *uneven-based*. Leaves are 2"- 3" long and triangular, teeth mostly *few to none*, and leafstalks *1/8"-1/4"* in length. Twigs *brown, rounded,* and *hairy;* pith *chambered* or solid only at the leaf nodes. Visible bud scales only *3-4*. Flowers inconspicuous; fruits small, brown, *one-seeded* spheres with a thin, somewhat-sweet covering. Fruitstalks are *longer* than leafstalks. Height to 50'. Dry slopes and streamsides, ranging from n-cen. Washington, n. Idaho, and n-cen. Nebraska to s. California, s-cen. Texas, and n. Mexico. Often called Western Hackberry or Sugarberry.

Southern Hackberry (*Celtis laevigata* Willd.) is similar but with leaves 2"- 6" in length and stalks *1/4"- 1/2"* long. Fruitstalks are *shorter* than leafstalks. From w. Texas eastward to the se. United States.

CALIFORNIA REDBUD *Cercis occidentalis* Torr. ex Gray
Leaves 2"- 5" long, deeply *heart-shaped* to nearly round, somewhat leathery, and the tips *blunt*. Leaf edges smooth, *not* toothed. Twigs hairless; often showing 1-3 lines descending from the leaf scars. Buds have *many* scales. Pith *continuous*. Short-stemmed, red-purple, half-inch blossoms outline the branchlets before the leaves come out, providing *showy* springtime displays. Flowers, not buds, are reddish. Mature fruits flat, brown *pods,* 2"- 3" long, *5/8"- 3/4"* wide, July-August or longer. Flowers reported sometimes to be eaten in salads. Dried red branch wood is used in basketry; the roots yield a red dye. Local, s. Utah, n. and cen. Arizona.

Eastern Redbud (*Cercis canadensis* L.) ranges westward to w. Texas and extreme se. New Mexico as var. *texensis* (Wats.) Hopkins. Closely resembling California Redbud but with leaves more *pointed* and fruit pods *under 1/2"* in width.

Plate 24

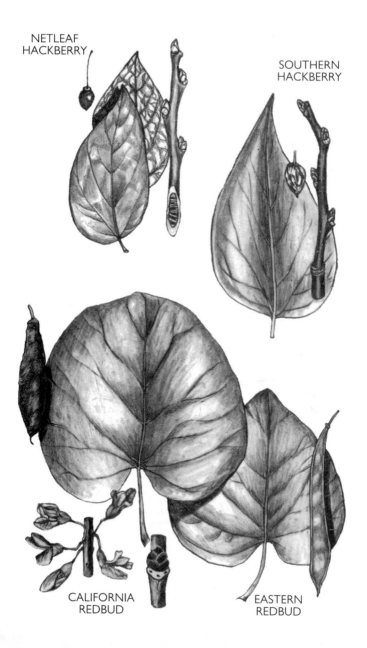

NETLEAF
HACKBERRY

SOUTHERN
HACKBERRY

CALIFORNIA
REDBUD

EASTERN
REDBUD

25. POPLARS: Aspen, Cottonwoods

The common names vary but all are closely related poplars. Leaves are broadly rounded or triangular, *long-stalked,* and often with 3-5 main veins meeting at the base (but see Narrowleaf Cottonwood). The lowermost bud scale is *directly above the leaf scar;* flowers and fruits are in catkins. Trunks are often smooth and whitish when young. Several species have *flattened* leafstalks.

QUAKING ASPEN *Populus tremuloides* Michx.
   Leaves 2"- 6" long, *fine-toothed,* often *nearly circular,* and becoming golden in autumn. Leafstalks *flattened,* enabling foliage to flutter in a breeze. Twigs *dark brown* with the end bud *smooth* and only 1/4"- 3/8" long. Young bark *chalk-white to greenish.* Height to 75'. A widespread tree in the western mountains from n. Alaska to Mexico. Quaking Aspens spread mostly by clonal root sprouts and estimates are made that some groves have survived for 10,000 years (far longer than other trees traditionally recognized as being long-lived - see Plate 3).

FREMONT COTTONWOOD *Populus fremontii* Wats.
   Ranging south from nw. Colorado and cen. Nevada, this is a tree of the Southwest. Leaves are *coarse-toothed,* mostly *triangular,* 2"- 5" long, and generally with a tapered tip. Leafstalks *flattened.* Twigs *yellowish,* with the end bud smooth and *3/8"- 1/2"* long. Mature trunk dark with deep grooves. Moist sites. To 100' tall. John C. Frémont, was a 19th century explorer and politician.

EASTERN COTTONWOOD (*P. deltoides* Bartr.) is similar but extends east from sw. Alberta, e. Colorado, and ne. New Mexico with *glands* at the leaf base and the end bud longer and *gummy.* Trees with intermediate characteristics and called Lanceleaf Cottonwood are considered hybrids with the following species.

NARROWLEAF COTTONWOOD *Populus angustifolia* James
   Much like willows (Plates 30-32) in foliage and habitat but the shiny buds have *several* scales. Leaves *narrow,* 3"- 5" long, 1"- 2" wide, *fine-toothed, feather-veined;* the slender foliage unique among our poplars. Leafstalks ± rounded but flattened on top and only *3/8"–1"* long. Twigs yellowish, hairless; end bud 1/4"– 1/2" long and sticky. Young bark rather smooth and whitish, becoming darker and furrowed. To 60' tall. Ranging mainly in the Rocky Mountains from sw. Alberta to n. Mexico.

Naturalized European species: White Poplar (*P. alba* L.) has 2"- 6" leaves either triangular or lobed and maplelike. Foliage, twigs, and buds *white-wooly.* **Lombardy Poplar** (*P. nigra* var. *italica* Muenchh.) is a tall, thin, *columnar* tree often planted for ornament.

Plate 25

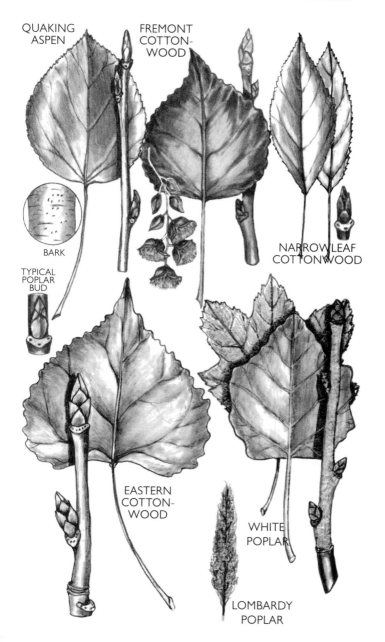

QUAKING ASPEN

FREMONT COTTON-WOOD

BARK

TYPICAL POPLAR BUD

NARROWLEAF COTTONWOOD

EASTERN COTTON-WOOD

WHITE POPLAR

LOMBARDY POPLAR

26. END BUDS CLUSTERED plus ACORNS: Oaks I

Despite varied foliage, oaks (Plates 26-28) are our only trees with *end buds clustered* at the twig tips and *more than three* bundle scars per leaf scar. Oaks also, of course, bear *acorn* fruits. In late spring, male blossoms occur in slender, *drooping* catkins several inches long; female flowers are small and unobtrusive. Acorns, green at first, become brown when mature. They are held in basal *cups* that, nevertheless, are commonly described as either bowl-shaped or saucerlike. Jumping-bean Sapium (Plate 33) also may have buds clustered at or near the twig ends but it differs otherwise.

An oak species is often classified as a member of either the white or red oak group. The lobe and leaf tips of white oaks *lack* the protruding hairlike *bristles* that are present in red oaks. Also, the acorns of white oaks require only one year to mature while those of red oaks take two. Thus white oak acorns grow *only* on the twigs while red oaks may have developing acorns on the twigs *as well as* older ones on the branchlets. In addition, the inner surface of the shells (not cups) of white oak acorns are *hairless* while those of red oaks are ± *hairy*. Still further, the meat of white oak acorns is light-colored and more edible in contrast to that of red oaks which usually contains much dark tannic acid and is bitter. Canyon Live Oak (Plate 27) and Emory Oak (Plate 28) are exceptions to some of these guidelines and are called intermediate oaks (see Plate 27).

The trees of this plate have somewhat leathery yet *deciduous* foliage, the leaves being either *lobed* or *toothed:* Most are white oaks.

GAMBEL OAK *Quercus gambelii* Nutt.
> The only oak in the central and southern Rockies with deeply-lobed foliage. Leaves 2"- 6" long. From n. Utah and s. Wyoming south to Mexico. Height to 65'. William Gambel collected Rocky Mountain plants in 1844.

WAVYLEAF OAK Often regarded as *Quercus undulata* Torr.
> An apparent complex of hybrids between Gambel Oak and either Havard, Chinkapin, Turbinella, Gray, Arizona, or Mohr oaks. Leaves 1"- 3" long and variable, with deep lobes or large teeth.

Barely reaching our area: **Havard (Shin) Oak** (*Q. havardii* Rydb.) ranges from w. Oklahoma /nw. Texas to se. New Mexico, the leaves 2"- 4" long, shallow-lobed, wavy-edged, or neither. **Chinkapin Oak** (*Q. muhlenbergii* Engelm.), an eastern tree, is also local in se. New Mexico and w. Texas with *thin* leaves sharply toothed. **Graves Oak** (*Q. gravesii* Sudw.), a *red* oak of w. Texas and ne. Mexico has non-leathery leaves with deep bristle-tipped lobes.

Plate 26

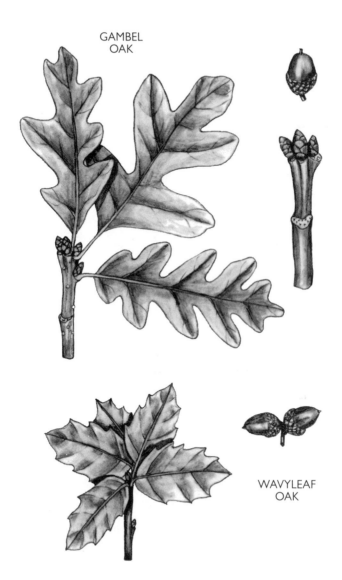

GAMBEL
OAK

WAVYLEAF
OAK

27. END BUDS CLUSTERED plus ACORNS: Oaks II

Other than the trees of Plate 26, oaks of the Southwest are *evergreen*. The oaks of this plate have leaves mostly only 1/2"- 2 1/2" long, leathery, *prickly-edged, and hollylike*. Twigs are usually hairy (use lens) and acorn cups mostly bowl-shaped. The first two species are members of the white oak group (see Plate 26); Canyon Live Oak is an intermediate oak (see below). The *crinkled* edges of Sandpaper Oak leaves are curled, crisped, or up-and-down wavy. Hollyleaf Buckthorn (Plate 22), Wavyleaf Oak (Plate 26), and oaks of Plate 28 have leaves sometimes prickly and often longer.

Oaks seldom grow large in the Southwest; elsewhere they are often valuable timber trees. Acorns are also important; they are essential in the diets of deer, squirrels, and other wildlife species. These fruits also once served as important foods for Native Americans. Even the bitter acorns of red oaks were rendered edible by grinding the kernels and treating the flour with hot water. Early settlers reportedly also used dried acorn shells as a coffee substitute. In Spanish, roble (ROHB-leh) is the general name for a deciduous oak species and encino (en-SEEN-oh) for an evergreen oak.

SANDPAPER OAK *Quercus pungens* Liebm.
 Usually shrubby but sometimes 25' tall. Foliage 3/4"- 2" long, *crinkled*, light- to *dark-green*, with *rough-hairy* (sandpapery) surfaces, and *V-shaped* bases. Occasionally lobed or without teeth. Acorns narrowly cylindrical, the cups on 1/16"-1/8" stalks. Rocky slopes, se. Arizona to cen. New Mexico and cen. Texas. Also n. Mexico. The specific name means sharp, prickly. Scrub Oak is another name for this and some other oaks.

TURBINELLA OAK *Quercus turbinella* Greene
 Foliage is *flat*, 1"- 2" long, dull *gray-green, hairless above*, usually fine-hairy beneath, the leaf bases ± *U-shaped*, and edges sometimes only slightly wavy. Distributed from s-cen. Colorado, s. Utah, s. Nevada, California to Arizona and New Mexico.

CANYON LIVE OAK *Quercus chrysolepis* Liebm.
 Leaves *1"- 2 1/2"* long, *flat*, often whitened or *yellowish* beneath, and somewhat *waxy*. Side veins are mostly *parallel*. Acorn cups deep, thick-walled, and often *gold-hairy*. Called an intermediate oak because, like a red oak, the fruits require two years to mature and have hairy inner acorn shells (not cups). They grow, however, on wood that does not normally produce new growth the second year and thus *appear* to mature on twigs like white oaks. To 60' tall. Ranges mainly in California, local in cen. and se. Arizona. The dense wood once was made into wedges and mauls (heavy hammers) to split logs. Also called Maul Oak The term live oak refers to the evergreen foliage (see Plate 28).

Plate 27

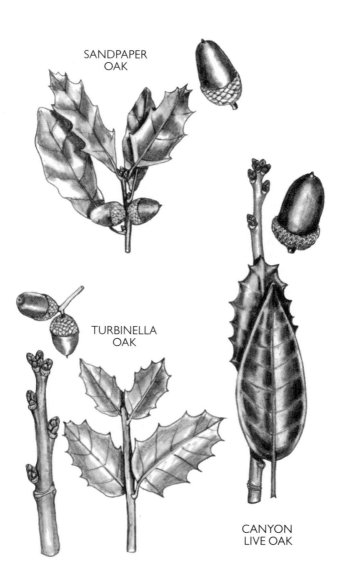

SANDPAPER
OAK

TURBINELLA
OAK

CANYON
LIVE OAK

28. END BUDS CLUSTERED plus ACORNS: Oaks III

Called live oaks because of their *evergreen* foliage, the species of this plate have leaves thick, ± leathery, toothed or not, but *seldom* prickly-edged. Most have longer leaves than those shown on Plate 27. Twigs mostly hairy. Only Emory Oak is not a white oak.

The first two species have dull leaf surfaces; the others have mostly shiny foliage. A few species have veins much raised on the leaf undersides. Acorn cups are mostly bowl-shaped and short-stalked.

The first three species range from mid-Arizona /New Mexico /w. Texas to Mexico. See also Plate 29.

GRAY OAK *Quercus grisea* Sarg.
An oak with *dull-surfaced,* grayish leaves *1"- 3"* long, tips *pointed,* bases U- or heart-shaped, and teeth few or none. Acorns 1/2"– 3/4" long, stalks to 1 1/4" in length, cup bowl-shaped. Height to 65'. Rocky slopes and canyons. Hybrids with Turbinella, Arizona, and Mohr oaks are known.

ARIZONA OAK *Quercus arizonica* Sarg.
Also with *dull* foliage but leaves *1"- 4"* in length, mostly *blunt, widest near the tip,* with *veins prominent* beneath. Acorns 1/4"– 3/4" long; cup stalks 3/4" long or none. Trunk bark thick. Height to 65'. Rocky slopes, cen. Arizona /cen. New Mexico /w. Texas to cen. Mexico. Often called Arizona White Oak. Intergrades with Gray and Turbinella oaks are common. Sometimes regarded as a part of *Q. grisea.*

EMORY OAK *Quercus emoryi* Torr. in W. H. Emory
Leaves 1"- 3" (4") long, *narrow,* hairless, *pointed,* and *shiny green on both sides* (often evident even at a distance). Tufts of white hairs frequently present at the base of the midrib; leaves occasionally toothed or prickly. An intermediate oak with hairy inner acorn shells (not cups), and nuts maturing in one year on the apparent (see Canyon Live Oak, Plate 27) twigs. Fruits 1/2"– 3/4" long. Height to 80". Possibly the most abundant oak in the boundary region. Henry Emory explored the Mexican border region in early 1800s. Hybridizes with Graves (Pl. 26) and Chisos (Plate 29) oaks.

MOHR OAK *Quercus mohriana* Buckl. ex Rydb.
A thicket-forming oak ranging from ne. New Mexico and cen. Oklahoma to nw. and cen. Texas and n. Mexico. Foliage *egg-shaped,* 1"- 4" long, shiny above, and *white-hairy beneath.* Acorns 1/4–1/2 in. long; cup bowl-like. Height to 20 ft. Hills and plains. Charles Mohr was a naturalist of the late 1800s.

Plate 28

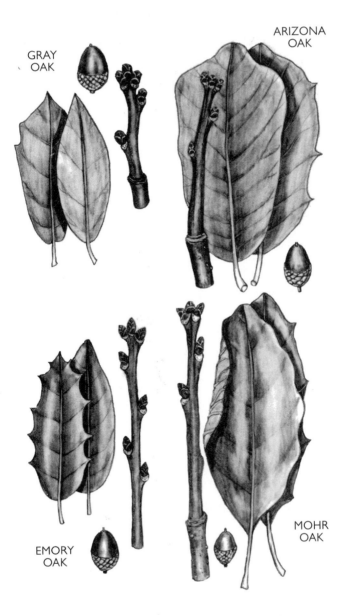

GRAY
OAK

ARIZONA
OAK

EMORY
OAK

MOHR
OAK

29. END BUDS CLUSTERED plus ACORNS: Oaks IV

The oaks of this group occur in the United States only within about 100 miles of the boundary with Mexico. Most are distributed from se. Arizona to w. Texas and n. Mexico. Twigs are mostly hairless. The first three species are white oaks; the others are red oaks. Most aspects of the first paragraph of Plate 28 also apply to this group.

NETLEAF OAK *Quercus rugosa* Née
Occurs from cen. Arizona, sw. New Mexico, and w. Texas to s. Mexico. Leaves 1"– 3" long and only half as wide, *dark* green, shiny, mostly *convex* above, hairy or not, usually toothed near the *broad* tip, veins *much raised* beneath and sunken above, base rounded or heart-shaped. Twigs mostly hairy. Acorns 1/2"– 1" long and on *1"–3"* stalks, cups bowl-shaped. Trunk bark thick. Canyons above 6000' elevation, tree size mainly in Mexico.

MEXICAN BLUE OAK *Quercus oblongifolia* Torr.
An oak with leaves only *1"- 2"* long, shiny, blue-gray, *blunt, parallel-sided,* hairless, *without* teeth. Acorns 1/2"– 3/4" long; cup bowl-like. Height to 30'. Mainly at4500'- 6000' elevations.

TOUMEY OAK *Quercus toumeyi* Sarg.
With the smallest leaves of any American oak, this species has foliage only *1/2"– 1 1/2"* long, hairless, shiny above, rarely few-toothed, with *pointed* tip and rounded base. Twigs hairy. Branchlet bark *flaky,* rough. Acorns 1/2"–5/8" long; cup bowl-shaped. Height to 30'. At 4000'– 7000' elevations. James W. Toumey, of the U. S. Forest Service, found the species in 1894.

SILVERLEAF OAK *Quercus hypoleucoides* A. Camus
A red oak with leaves narrow, 1"- 4" long, *dark green* and shiny above, thickly white- or *silvery-hairy* and veiny beneath, *pointed* at the tip, the edges *rolled under* and with no teeth or only a few bristly ones. Acorns 1/2"–5/8"long; cup bowl-shaped. Height to 60'. Slopes at 5000'–7000' elevations south from e-cen. Arizona. An attractive species often used in landscaping.

CHISOS OAK *Quercus graciliformis* C. H. Muller
Found only in the Chisos Mountains of w. Texas, a red oak with *narrow* leaves 3"– 4" long, 3/4"– 1 1/4" wide, long-pointed, V-based, *thin* but ± leathery, shiny above, hairless and somewhat *copper-colored* beneath, *drooping,* with 5–10 *large* bristle-tipped teeth or shallow lobes, or teeth lacking.Twigs hairy or not. Acorns narrow, 5/8" long, 3/8" wide; cup saucerlike. Height to 25'. Slopes, about 5500' elevation. Hybridizes with Emory Oak.

LATELEAF OAK *Quercus tardifolia* C. H. Muller Not shown.
A red oak with thick, leathery, blue-green leaves reported as local in the Chisos Mountains but its validity is uncertain.

Plate 29

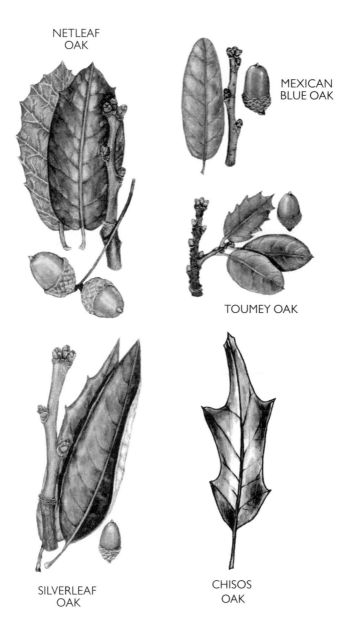

NETLEAF
OAK

MEXICAN
BLUE OAK

TOUMEY OAK

SILVERLEAF
OAK

CHISOS
OAK

30. BUDS WITH ONE SCALE: Willows I

Though some willows can be recognized by their *slender* leaves, others have wider foliage [and some non-willows (Plate 33) also have narrow leaves]. All willows, however, have buds with *only one scale,* the scale edges mostly fused (overlapping in four species), use lens. Twigs are mostly hairless; bundle scars are *three;* the end bud is false. Flowers and fruits are present in spring and early summer in slender, dry, caterpillarlike *catkins.* Trunks are dark and rough.

Vegetative characters are variable; hybrids common; identification often difficult. Willows tend to grow on moist sites; many are shrubby. Arizona Sycamore (Plate 23), also with a single bud scale, is otherwise different. See also Narrowleaf Cottonwood (Plate 25).

Willow twigs are eaten by deer, elk, rabbits, hares, and many rodents. Salicin, a chemical derived from willow bark, is the original substance from which aspirin was developed.

The trees of this plate have leaves *very narrow* (8-15 times longer than wide) and mostly 2"- 6" long. Leaves are often whitened beneath, leafstalks are generally *without* glands, and stipules are usually *small* or absent. Leaf bases are mostly *V-shaped.* Most species have gray-green foliage. Except for some specimens of Sandbar and Yewleaf willows, the leaf edges are *fine-toothed.*

SANDBAR WILLOW *Salix exigua* Nutt.
  A streamside species with *very* narrow leaves only *1/8"- 1/2"* wide and short- or *long-pointed* . Leaf undersides and twigs often *white-hairy.* Leaf teeth wide, often *few,* rarely none; stalks ± *1/8"* long. Buds to 1/4". To 20' tall. Nearly transcontinental, south from cen. Alaska. The long twigs /branchlets can be woven into baskets.

GOODDING WILLOW *Salix gooddingii* C. Ball
  Leaves fine-toothed, short-pointed, and *green* beneath. Leafstalks ± 1/4" long with *glands* present at or near the leaf base. Twigs *yellowish* and ± hairy; buds to 1/8". The edges of the single bud scale are *not fused* but show as a line on the smooth bud (see Plate 32). Southwestern states and nearby Mexico.

YEWLEAF WILLOW *Salix taxifolia* Kunth.
  A desert tree with gray-hairy leaves only *1/2"- 1 3/4"* long, 1/8"- 3/8" wide, and short-pointed. Twigs hairy, often drooping. Height 40'. Se. Arizona /New Mexico /w. Texas to Guatemala.

Weeping Willow (*Salix babylonica* L.), often planted, is an Old World tree with *extremely* long twigs and branchlets that *hang vertically.* Leaves *long-pointed,* white-hairy beneath, teeth few or none, the edges turned under. Leafstalks to 1/2" with glands *present.* Buds to 1/8" in length. Height to 50'.

Plate 30

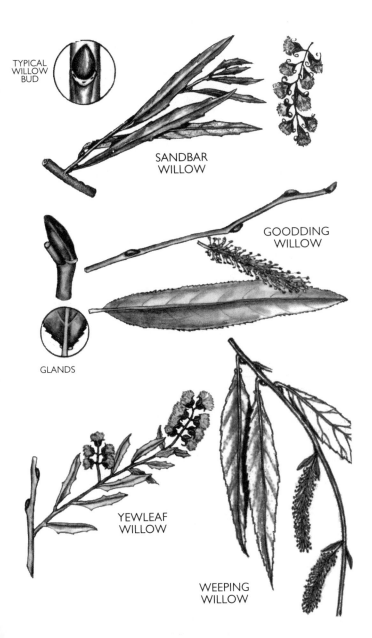

TYPICAL
WILLOW
BUD

SANDBAR
WILLOW

GOODDING
WILLOW

GLANDS

YEWLEAF
WILLOW

WEEPING
WILLOW

31. BUDS WITH ONE SCALE: WILLOWS II

The willows of this plate mostly have leaves *without teeth* and leaf bases *V-shaped*. (Note: The leaves of Bebb Willow only sometimes lack teeth.) The first two species have leaves of medium width (length 5-7 times width); the last two have wider foliage (2-4 times longer than broad). For willows in general, see Plate 30.

GEYER WILLOW *Salix geyeriana* Anderss.
Leaves often blunt, silky-hairy, only *1"- 3"* long, *3/8"- 1/2"* wide and ± whitened beneath. Twigs somewhat reddish, often with a whitish powder; buds *less than 1/8"* long. Height to 15'. At 5000'-7000' elevations from s. British Columbia to ne.Utah and cen. Colorado. Also w-cen. Nevada, the Sierra Nevada, and cen. Arizona. Karl Geyer was a German botanist who collected plants in the West during the 1840s.

ARROYO WILLOW *Salix lasiolepis* Benth.
Leaves short-pointed or blunt, *2"- 5"* long, *1/2"- 1"* wide, *shiny,* whitish beneath, rather *leathery,* and ± *thickened.* Twigs ± hairless, yellowish; buds *over 1/4"* long. Height to 30'. Mainly below 7000'. Widespread in the coast ranges; local inland from n-cen. Washington to n-cen. New Mexico and nw. Mexico.

SCOULER WILLOW *Salix scouleriana* J. Baratt ex Hook.
Leaves mostly blunt, *2"- 5"* long, *1/2"- 1 1/2"* wide, *shiny,* and more or less wavy-edged. Foliage *widest toward the tip,* whitish and often somewhat hairy beneath. Twigs yellowish to dark and usually *drooping;* buds *over 1/4"* long. Height to 25'. Ranging mainly in the Pacific Northwest and prairie provinces of Canada but also in the Rockies south to Arizona and New Mexico. John Scouler, a Scottish physician, studied plants along the Pacific Coast in the early 19th century.

BEBB WILLOW *Salix bebbiana* Sarg.
Leaves *2"- 3"* long, *1/2"- 1"* wide, mostly pointed, whitish- or *gray-hairy,* with teeth *coarse* or none. Twigs *gray-hairy,* tending to branch *at wide angles* from the branchlets; buds 1/8"-1/4" long. Wood used for charcoal. The long withes (twigs /branchlets) may be woven into baskets. Throughout the Rocky Mountains from cen. Alaska to Arizona and New Mexico; transcontinental in the north.

Plate 31

GEYER
WILLOW

ARROYO
WILLOW

TYPICAL
WILLOW
BUD

SCOULER
WILLOW

BEBB
WILLOW

32. BUDS WITH ONE SCALE: WILLOWS III

These species have leaves of *medium width* (5-7 times longer than wide). Leaves *fine-toothed,* hairless, *whitened* beneath, mostly *long-pointed,* bases generally *U-shaped,* stalks mainly 1/2"- 3/4" long without glands (use lens). Twigs usually hairless and winter buds mostly *under 1/8"* long. Unlike most willows, Bonpland, Red, and Peachleaf willows have the edges of the single bud scale *not fused* but showing as a line on the smooth bud (see also Goodding Willow, Plate 30).

On Plate 31, Geyer and Arroyo willows also have leaves regularly of medium width but without teeth while Bebb Willow may have coarse teeth.

See Plate 29 for characterics of willows as a group. Narrowleaf Cottonwood (Plate 25) is quite willowlike.

PACIFIC WILLOW *Salix lucida* ssp. *lasiandra* (Benth.) E. Murray
Leaves 2"- 5" long, 1/2"- 1" wide, *shiny,* dark green above. Leafstalks 1/2"- 3/4" long with *glands present.* Buds *over 1/4"* in length. In the Rockies from cen. Alaska and cen. Yukon to Arizona and New Mexico. Formerly *Salix lasiandra* Benth. Useful for making charcoal.

BONPLAND WILLOW *Salix bonplandiana* Kunth.
Leaves firm, ± *thick,* 3"- 7" long, 1/2"- 1 1/2" wide, mostly *shiny* above, long- or short-pointed, either U- or V-based, the stalks 1/4"- 1/2" in length and *not* glandular. Leaves often quite narrow. Twigs reddish, mostly *hairless;* buds *1/8"- 1/4"* long. From se. Arizona to Guatemala.

RED WILLOW *Salix laevigata* Bebb   Not shown
Like Bonpland Willow but wider ranging and the twigs mostly *hairy.* Leafstalk glands *present or not.* Occurs from s. Oregon and California to cen. Arizona and Mexico.

PEACHLEAF WILLOW *Salix amygdaloides* Anders.
A widespread willow with leaves 3/4"- 1 1/4" wide, yellow-green, and mostly *dull-surfaced.* Leafstalk glands *present.* Twigs brown to *orange,* ± *drooping.* From se. British Columbia, ne. Nevada, ne. Arizona, and w. Texas to e. North America.

White Willow (*Salix alba* L.), a European tree widely planted, has leaves *white-hairy* on both sides and leafstalk glands *present.*

Plate 32

PACIFIC
WILLOW

BONPLAND
WILLOW

TYPICAL
WILLOW
BUD

GLANDS

PEACHLEAF
WILLOW

33. NON-WILLOWS WITH NARROW LEAVES

Except for Torrey Vauquelinia, the leaves of species on this plate are *deciduous* and *not toothed.* There is only *one* bundle scar. See also Narrowleaf Cottonwood (Plate 25), Silverleaf Oak (Plate 29), Black Cherry (Plate 35), Arizona Madrone (Plate 38), and Curlleaf Cercocaarpus (Plate 39). These narrow-leaved species all lack the single, smooth bud scale and three bundle scars of willows.

RUSSIAN-OLIVE *Elaeagnus angustifolia* L.

A Eurasian import widely planted for ornament and as a drought-resistant windbreak. Leaves 1"- 4" long, 1/2"- 1" wide, short-pointed, U- or V-based, green above, and *silver-scaly* beneath. Plant often thorny, twigs *silver-white.* Flowers yellowish, spring; fruits egg-shaped, ± fleshy, silver-red to white. Height to 25'. Frequently called Oleaster. Fruits eaten by many birds and mammals. Silver Buffaloberry (Plate 12) has opposite leaves. When thorns are present, compare Plate 22.

DESERT-WILLOW *Chilopsis linearis* (Cav.) Sweet

An arid-zone tree or shrub with leaves 3"- 7" long and *only 1/8"- 1/4" wide.* Foliage long-pointed, V-based, *green* on both sides, parallel-sided, and hairless. Some leaves may be opposite or in whorls of three. Twigs long, hairless, slender; buds tiny, at right angles to the twigs. Flowers showy, white to purple, 1"- 1 1/2" long, April-August; fruits slim, 4"- 12" long, dry, brown capsules, parts of which may remain in winter. Height to 35'. Desert washes, from s. California, sw. Utah, and w. Texas south into Mexico.

JUMPING-BEAN SAPIUM *Sapium biloculare* (Wats.) Pax.

The only species in this group with *milky* sap or *spur branches.* Leaves 1"- 2" long, 3/8"- 5/8" wide, *fine-toothed, U-based,* and mainly clustered near the twig ends. Flowers small, without petals, in slender spikes, March-November; fruits dry, half-inch long, 2-lobed capsules. Height to 20'. Desert washes, sw. Arizona and nw. Mexico. Fruits often occupied by insect larvae whose movements cause the capsules to "jump". Like other euphorbia family members, the milky sap causes skin irritation and is poisonous when swallowed. Formerly used by native peoples to stun fish and to poison arrows (practices that are now illegal).

TORREY VAUQUELINIA *Vauquelinia californica* (Torr.) Sarg.

An *evergreen* tree or shrub with *leathery* leaves 2"- 4" long, 1/4"- 1/2" wide, hairy beneath, short-pointed, V-based, the parallel edges *coarse-toothed.* Flowers small, white, June; fruits dry, hairy, 1/4" long, oval capsules, August. Height to 20'. Mountain slopes to 5000' elevation, s. Arizona and Baja California. When the species was named, the borders of California had not been established.

Plate 33

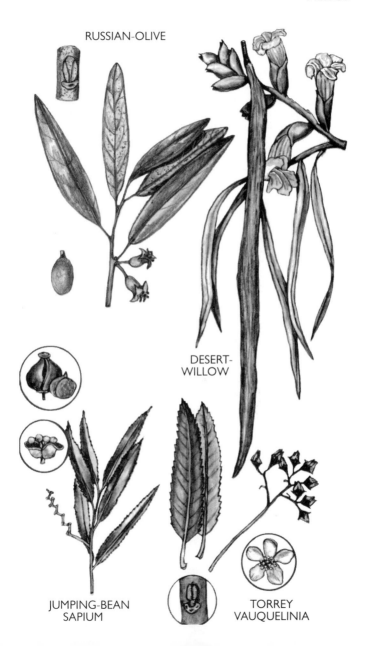

RUSSIAN-OLIVE

DESERT-
WILLOW

JUMPING-BEAN
SAPIUM

TORREY
VAUQUELINIA

34. LEAVES DOUBLE-TOOTHED:
Alders, Water Birch, Knowlton Hornbeam

Trees with short-pointed leaves, the major teeth also toothed.

Alders grow mostly on damp sites with mature female catkins brown and woody like *inch-long pine cones.* Leaves are mostly *hairless,* 2"- 5" long, the main veins parallel. Buds mostly *stalked, reddish, blunt,* 1/4"-3/8" long, and with 2-3 scales *not* overlapping. Alders are among the few non-legumes that bear root nodules whose bacteria can convert atmospheric nitrogen into soil-enriching compounds. Powdered alder bark makes an orange-red dye and is said to control both diarrhea and external bleeding. **Water Birch** and **Knowlton Hornbeam** differ from alders as described. Deer, beavers, and porcupines eat the twigs or inner bark of all four species; several grouse species feed on the buds.

MOUNTAIN ALDER *Alnus incana* ssp. *tenuifolia* (Nutt.) Breit.
Leaves with deep teeth, *6-9* pairs of side veins, and bases mostly *U-shaped.* Buds *1/4"- 3/8"* long, with some *not always* stalked. Trunk bark gray, often with short, *scattered,* horizontal lines. Cones 3/8"- 5/8" long. Height to 30'. Mountain slopes from cen. Yukon and w-cen. Alaska to e. Arizona and w. New Mexico. Formerly named *Alnus tenuifolia.* Also called Thinleaf Alder.

ARIZONA ALDER *Alnus oblongifolia* Torr.
Like Mountain Alder but leaves with *9-13* side veins and usually *V-shaped* bases. Buds *to 1/2"* long. Height to 60'. Cen. Arizona to n. Mexico, local in n. and cen. New Mexico.

WATER BIRCH *Betula occidentalis* Hook.
A birch whose *red-brown, shiny* trunk is marked with *crowded* white transverse streaks. Leaves *1"- 3"* long, *short-pointed,* often heart-shaped, with *4-5* pairs of side veins. Twigs *rough-warty,* hairless with spur branches *present;* buds *pointed,* with only *2-3 overlapping* scales. The tiny fruits are in slim, *non-woody* catkins. Height to 40'. Local throughout the western mountains south to n. Arizona and n. New Mexico. Many cherries (Plate 35) have spur branches and young bark streaked brown, but their foliage is single-toothed..

KNOWLTON HORNBEAM *Ostrya knowltonii* Cov.
Though related, this species *lacks* the streaked trunk, spur branches, few-scaled buds, and slender catkins of Water Birch. The 1"- 3" leaves of this species are *egg-shaped.* Twigs are more or less *hairy;* buds are *pointed* with *6-8* scales. Fruits *inflated,* bladderlike, papery, and *clustered.* Height to 30'. Moist canyons, se. Utah and nw. Arizona to w. Texas.

Plate 34

MOUNTAIN
ALDER

ARIZONA
ALDER

MATURE
FEMALE
CATKINS

IMMATURE
FEMALE
CATKINS

WATER
BIRCH

KNOWLTON
HORNBEAM

35. LEAVES SINGLE-TOOTHED: Cherries

Cherries have *short-pointed* leaves 2"- 6" long and trunks mostly marked by thin *horizontal lines* (see also Mountain Alder and Water Birch, Plate 34). Buds have *several* scales and leaf bases or leafstalks mostly bear one or two tiny *glands*. Twigs are mostly hairless, often with a *sour* or almond odor when broken. Springtime flowers are small and white; fruits are spherical, *fleshy*, and *single-seeded*. American Plum (Plate 22) is a thorny relative. These wild cherries have finely *single-toothed* foliage, mostly with sharp tips.

BITTER CHERRY *Prunus emarginata* (Hook.) Walp.
Leaves 1"- 3" long, sometimes narrow, tips usually *round-pointed,* and teeth rather *blunt.* Spur branches *present;* flowers /fruits in *short, rounded* groups. Fruits 1/4"- 1/3", red to black, the calyx lobes[1] *deciduous.* Height 60'- 80' (100'). From British Columbia and Montana south to cen. and se. Arizona /sw. New Mexico. Often in thickets. Many animals eat the fruits despite the taste that we perceive as bitter; mule deer browse the twigs.

CHOKE CHERRY *Prunus virginiana* var. *demissa* (Nutt.) Torr.
Along with Black Cherry, flowers /fruits are in *slender, 2"- 4" long clusters* and spur branches are *lacking.* Foliage is 2"- 5" long, *egg-shaped,* and *sharp-toothed.* There are 8-11 lateral vein pairs, the midrib is *hairless,* and leafstalks are often reddish. Buds are *more* than 1/4" long with scale tips *rounded.* Flowers May-June; fruits purple to black, the calyx lobes *deciduous,* July-October. Height to 30'. Thickets and woods, from British Columbia and Newfoundland to s. California, Arizona, New Mexico, w. Texas, and Virginia. The tart fruits often used for pies and jelly; also much eaten by wildlife. Frequently listed as *P. demissa.*

BLACK CHERRY *Prunus serotina* Ehrh.
Like Choke Cherry but with leaves more *narrow,* 2"- 6" long, teeth *incurved or blunt,* side veins *more than 13 pairs,* and the midrib often *hairy-fringed* beneath. Buds *under 3/16"* long, the scales *pointed.* Fruits *blackish, retaining* calyx lobes, June-October. Height 60'- 80' (100'). Woods and thickets throughout the East, local from Arizona /New Mexico to cen. Texas. Lumber valuable for furniture and home interiors; the fruits can be made into jelly.

---

[1]The calyx is the circle of green modified leaves (sepals) that surrounds the flower petals. When dry on the fruit, sepals are tan or brown.

Plate 35

BITTER
CHERRY

BARK

CHOKE
CHERRY

BLACK
CHERRY

36. LEAVES SINGLE-TOOTHED :
Serviceberries /Birchleaf Buckthorn /Siberian Elm

Unlike the cherries of Plate 35, horizontal lines on the trunk, glands on the leafstalk, and distinctive odors from broken twigs are *lacking*. Except for Siberian Elm, fruits are fleshy and *several-seeded.*

WESTERN SERVICEBERRY *Amelanchier alnifolia* (Nutt.) Nutt.
A small tree or shrub, the leaves *nearly circular, 1"- 3"* long, with *7-9* pairs of side veins and 3-20 pairs of *coarse teeth* mainly *toward the leaf tip.* Leafstalks *1/2"- 1"* long. Buds *scaly;* purplish; spur branches usually *present.* Flowers attractive,*white,* clustered, with petals 3/8"- 5/8" long; April-June; fruits juicy, *purplish,* edible, 1/4"- 1/2" wide; June-August. Height to 42'. Found from n-cen. Alaska, ne. Manitoba and w. Minnesota to nw. California, n. Arizona, nw. New Mexico. The origin and meaning of the Serviceberry name are uncertain, though possibly derived from Sorbusberry [a European mountain-ash (*Sorbus*) is called Servicetree]. Saskatoon Juneberry, Western Juneberry, and Alderleaf Juneberry are other names.

UTAH JUNEBERRY *Amelanchier utahensis* Koehne
A shrub or low tree similar to Western Serviceberry but leaves only *1/2"- 1 1/4"* long, including *1/4"- 1/2"* stalks. Flower petals only 1/8"- 1/4" long; fruits just 1/8"- 1/4" in diameter. Slopes and canyons, scattered localities from s. Oregon, cen. Idaho and sw. Montana south to Mexico.

BIRCHLEAF BUCKTHORN *Rhamnus betulifolia* Greene
This small tree has leaves *3"- 6"* long, 1"– 2 1/2" wide, *fine-toothed* near the *mostly-rounded* tip, and with 7- 10 pairs of *markedly parallel* veins prominent beneath. Twigs often slightly hairy, spur branches *lacking,* buds *without* scales. Flowers May–June; fruits black, July–October. Height to 20'. At 4000'- 7000' elevations from s. Nevada, s. Utah, and w. Texas to n. Mexico.

SIBERIAN ELM *Ulmus pumila* L.
Unlike most elms (mainly in the East), these leaves are *single-toothed* with bases *even.* Buds small, *4-scaled,* and ± blunt; flower buds *enlarged,* nearly *black,* conspicuous in late winter. Flowers and fruits small, the former lacking petals; fruits *papery,* winged, almost-circular, 1-seeded. An import from Asia, often planted for windbreaks and occasionally escaping. Often called Chinese Elm, but that name is more properly applied to the fall-flowering *U. parviflora* Jacq. naturalized mainly in the se. United States. As in all elms, the inner bark is fibrous. With a knife-cut, it can be pulled away in strips (useful for fishing lines, snares, etc.).

Plate 36

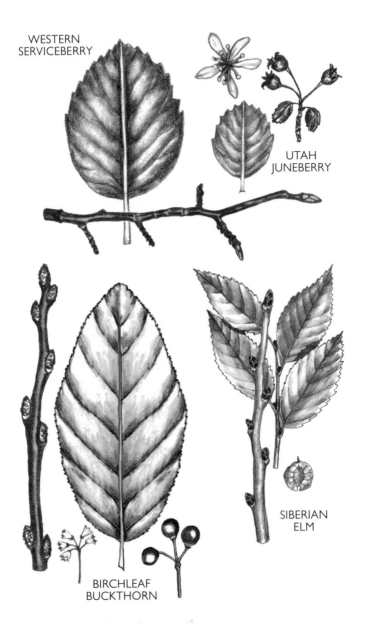

WESTERN
SERVICEBERRY

UTAH
JUNEBERRY

BIRCHLEAF
BUCKTHORN

SIBERIAN
ELM

37. LEAVES EVERGREEN, MOSTLY TOOTHED OR LOBED

Birchleaf Cercocarpus has *single-toothed* foliage, Hairy Cercocarpus has leaves *mostly* single-toothed, while Cliffrose has leafage with 3-5 small *lobes*. These three species have tiny fruits with attractive, long, *feathery tails*. Big Sagebrush is different. All plants of this plate show numerous spur branches. See also Torrey Vauquelinia (Plate 33).

BIRCHLEAF CERCOCARPUS *Cercocarpus betuloides* Torr. & Gray
Leaves *3/4"- 1 1/2"* in length, *parallel-veined, V-based,* often *velvet-hairy* beneath, *toothed above the middle,* and leaf edges *flat.* Buds *scaly.* Flowers greenish, 1/4" wide in *clusters* of 2-5, March-May; fruits single-seeded, narrow, dry, with a *slender plume 1 1/2"- 4" long.* Height to 25'. Chapparal, from sw. Oregon along the coast to nw. Mexico; local in the Sierra Nevada and cen. Arizona. Sometimes named *C. montanus* Raf. Wood is heavy and will not float soon after being cut; it is often brownish and used in woodworking. Though also called Mountain-mahogany, it is not related to tropical mahoganies. The name cercocarpus is based on the Greek for "tailed fruit". In the absence of fruits, compare California Buckthorn (Plate 38). Curlleaf Cercocarpus (Plate 39) is related.

HAIRY CERCOCARPUS *Cercocarpus breviflorus* Gray
Similar to Birchleaf Cercocarpus but the leaves are *3/4"- 1 1/4"* long, some usually *without* teeth. Foliage *silky-hairy* beneath and the leaf edges *rolled under.* Flowers *single* (rarely in 2s or 3s), the fruit plumes only *1- 1 1/2"* long. Dry slopes, mid-elevations, n-cen. Arizona to w. Texas and n. Mexico.

CLIFFROSE *Purshia mexicana* var. *stansburyana* (Torr.) Welsh
An attractive small tree with leaves *3-5 lobed, only 1/4"- 1/2"* in length, *sticky, gland-dotted* (use lens), the *edges rolled under,* and *white-wooly* beneath. Leaf bases raised, hiding buds; twigs hairless. Flowers *showy,* white, about 1" across, clustered, spring; fruits with a *feathery tail 1"- 2" long,* autumn. Trunk shreddy. Height to 25'. Dry, rocky sites at 4000'-10,000' elevations, from n. Nevada and n. Utah to se. California, w. New Mexico and n-cen. Mexico. Formerly in the genus *Cowania.*

BIG SAGEBRUSH *Artemesia tridentata* Nutt.
A *gray-green* shrub (rarely a tree), widespread in semi-arid areas throughout the West. Leaves 1/2"- 2" long, *aromatic,* hairy, ± leathery, short-stalked, narrowly *wedge-shaped,* and with *3 (5) large end teeth.* Fruits tiny, dry, hairy. An important forage species for bighorn sheep, mule deer, and livestock. Leaves and buds are also eaten by sharptail, sage, and dusky grouse.

Plate 37

BIRCHLEAF
CERCOCARPUS

HAIRY
CERCOCARPUS

CLIFFROSE

BIG
SAGEBRUSH

38. LEAVES EVERGREEN mostly NOT TOOTHED

The foliage of these trees is thick, leathery, and only occasionally (especially in young plants) with the edges toothed. Spur branches lacking. In the first three species, the pith is narrow and the fruits are several-seeded.

ARIZONA MADRONE *Arbutus arizonica* (Gray) Sarg.

Leaves 2"- 4" long, 1/2"- 1" wide, the bases *V-* or, occasionally, heart-shaped. Buds *scaly.* Trunk bark *gray-furrowed.* Flowers small, white, bell-shaped, in branched groups, March-May; fruits red to orange, spherical, 1/4"- 1/2" wide, June-winter. Height to 30'. Slopes at 4000'- 8000' elevations from se. Arizona /sw. New Mexico south along Mexico's Sierra Madre. Bark and leaves are astringent. Wood makes good charcoal.

TEXAS MADRONE *Arbutus texana* Buckl.

Like Arizona Madrone but the leaves *U-based* and *3/4"-1 1/2"* wide. Trunk bark *reddish-smooth.* Found from se. New Mexico and cen. Texas to n. Mexico.

CALIFORNIA BUCKTHORN *Rhamnus californica* Eschsch.

With variable foliage and *rarely* attaining tree size, this species has leaves 2"- 4" long, 1/2"- 2" wide, often *whitish* or yellow beneath. The leaves have 7-11 pairs of *parallel* leaf veins, either U- or V-shaped bases, and are sometimes fine-toothed (rarely with rather coarse teeth). Leaves occasionally opposite. Buds *without* scales, *hairy.* Flowers greenish, March-April; fruits *black,* juicy, August-September. To 15' tall. Ranging mainly in California, from extreme sw. Oregon to n. Baja California, but also to cen. Arizona /sw. New Mexico. Also called California Coffeeberry. Hollyleaf Buckthorn (Plate 22) is related. When fruits are absent, compare Birchleaf Cercocarpus (Plate 37).

SUGAR SUMAC *Rhus ovata* Wats.

Leaves 3"- 4" long, 1 1/2"- 3" wide, U-based, mostly short-pointed, *tending to fold along the midrib,* and sometimes with a few coarse teeth. When crushed, the foliage has a pleasant resinous odor. Twigs soft; pith *wide, brown.* Buds small, hairy, *without* scales, nearly hidden by the leafstalk bases. Flowers whitish, in dense terminal clusters, March-May; fruits red-hairy, sticky, August-September. Height to 15'. Sw. California to Baja California, also cen. Arizona.

Plate 38

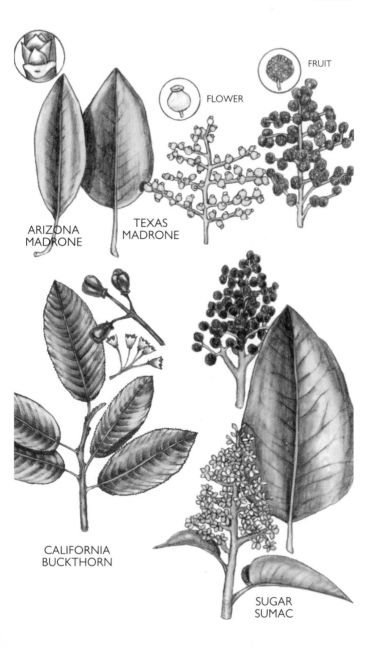

FLOWER

FRUIT

ARIZONA
MADRONE

TEXAS
MADRONE

CALIFORNIA
BUCKTHORN

SUGAR
SUMAC

39. LEAVES EVERGREEN NOT TOOTHED

Some evergreen trees of Plates 27, 28, and 38 also may lack leaf teeth.

CURLLEAF CERCOCARPUS *Cercocarpus ledifolius* Nutt.

A shrub or small tree of mountain slopes throughout the American West. Leaves only *1/2"- 1 1/2"* long, *narrow,* pointed at both ends, short-stalked, edges *curled under,* and sometimes hairy beneath. Spur branches *common.* Flowers without petals and inconspicuous. Fruits tiny but with interesting *feathery tails* 2"- 3" long. Mainly dry slopes, from se.Washingon /cen. Idaho /sw. Montana to s. California, n. Arizona, and sw. Colorado. Freshly-cut heartwood is heavy, brown, and will not float. It makes nice turned objects and leads to the alternate name of Mountain-mahogany. Mule deer browse the leaves and twigs. Birchleaf and Hairy cercocarpuses (Plate 37) are related.

PRINGLE MANZANITA *Arctostaphylos pringlei* Parry

Rarely reaching tree size, the trunk is *smooth, bare,* and *red-brown* (much the color and texture of Texas Madrone, Plate 38). Leaves *1"- 2"* long, ± *egg-shaped,* mostly hairless, somewhat whitened, and often with tiny tips. Twigs *sticky-hairy.* Flowers urn-shaped, *pink or white,* 1/4"- 3/8" long; fruits spherical, 1/4"- 3/8" in diameter, *fleshy or leathery,* mostly reddish, and ± glandular-hairy. Mountains of s. California, cen. Arizona, and n. Baja Calilfornia.

TREE TOBACCO *Nicotiana glauca* Graham

Introduced from South America for ornamental plantings but escaped and naturalized at elevations under 3000'. Leaves egg-shaped, 2"- 6" long, 1"- 4" wide, long-stalked, short-pointed or blunt, hairless, with a whitish bloom. Flowers yellow, to 1 1/2" long, tubular, clustered at twig ends; fruit capsules about 1/2" in length, dry, splitting, with many small seeds. A shrub or small tree often common along desert streambeds. To 20' in height. Near the Mexican boundary from s. California to s. Texas.

Plate 39

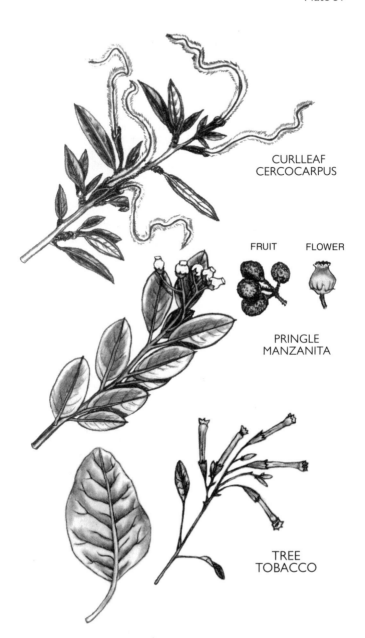

CURLLEAF
CERCOCARPUS

FRUIT   FLOWER

PRINGLE
MANZANITA

TREE
TOBACCO

VI. Yuccas, Palms, Cacti
Plates 40-42
40. YUCCAS I

Yuccas are characteristic plants of the Southwest with clusters of *evergreen, spine-tipped, bayonet-shaped, parallel-veined,*and mostly stiff leaves. Trunks often covered with dead leaves. Flowers in upright clusters, *showy, white,* with petals and petal-like sepals *over 1/2" long,* Fruits *fleshy, cylindrical capsules* several inches long, and usually drooping. Native Americans ate the buds, flowers, and flower stalks raw or roasted, and dried them for storage.The fibrous leaves were used for thatching, rope, sandals, coarse blankets, and baskets. Fruits are eaten by rabbits, rodents, and mule deer. Spanish-dagger is an alternate name. Also called Palma (PAL-ma) or Palmillo (pal-MEE-yo). See also *Nolina* below. For yuccas found wild in the United States only near the Mexican border, see Plate 41.

MOHAVE YUCCA *Yucca schidigera* K. E. Ortgies
Leaves *16"- 32"* long, *1"- 2"* wide, mostly *concave* above, with obvious free *marginal fibers.* Flower clusters *12"- 24"* tall, single flowers *1"- 2"* long, March-May. Fruits 3"- 4" in length, *thick and fleshy.* Trunk mostly leaf-covered. To 20' tall. Dry soils at 1000'- 5000' elevations, s. California, s. Nevada, and nw. Arizona to Baja California.

JOSHUATREE YUCCA *Yucca brevifolia* Engelm.
The most treelike of yuccas with leaves only *6"- 13"* long, *1/4"- 1/2"* wide, *flat* above, and the edges *fine-toothed* (test with fingernail). Flower clusters only *6"- 15"* tall, the blossoms *2"- 3"* in length, March-May. Fruits 2"- 4" long, the spongy walls becoming thin and dry but *not* splitting. Trunks much branched, often bare. Height to 50'. A characteristic species of the Mohave desert, at 2000'- 6000' elevations in se. California, s. Nevada, sw. Utah, and nw. Arizona.

SOAPTREE YUCCA *Yucca elata* Engelm.
A *narrow-leaved* yucca with leaves *12"- 35"* long, *1/8"- 5/16"* wide, *flat* above, flexible, and edges showing *separating fibers.* Flower clusters *3'- 7'* tall and single blossoms to 2" in length, May-July. Fruits 1 1/2"- 3" long, *thin-walled, dry, erect,* and *splitting open* when ripe. To 30' in height. Grasslands and deserts, 1500'- 6000' elevations from cen. Arizona, cen. New Mexico, and w. Texas to n. Mexico. Local in sw. Utah. Fluids of roots and stems have been used for soap by native peoples. Clipped foliage is often fed to livestock during droughts.

Bigelow Nolina [*Nolina bigelovii* (Torrey) S.Wats.] is a similar but ± shrubby plant (rarely 15' tall) with leaves *28"- 48"* long, *1/2"- 1 1/4"* wide, and *not* spine-tipped. Flowers less than 3/16" long. Occurs from nw. Arizona and se. California to nw. Mexico.

Plate 40

FLOWER

JOSHUATREE
YUCCA

SOAPTREE
YUCCA

MOHAVE
YUCCA

41. YUCCAS II

These yuccas occur only near the Mexican border from se. Arizona and s. New Mexico to s. Texas and nearby Mexico. Mostly, leaves are *over 2 1/2' long, more than 2" wide, smooth-concave* above, and edges with evident *loose fibers.* Most fruits fleshy, *not* splitting.

TORREY YUCCA *Yucca torreyi* Shafer
  Leaves *2'-5'* long, *2"- 3"* wide, thick, dull, *gray-green,* and *somewhat roughened* on both surfaces. Flower clusters *3'- 3 1/2'* long; single blossoms 2"- 3" in length, the petals and sepals[1] fused *only at the base*, March–April; fruits 4"- 6" long, fleshy. To 25 ft. tall, often not branched. Dry soils from s. New Mexico and w. Texas into n. Mexico. 19th-century botanist John Torrey of Columbia University described this plant. Locally called Palmapita (PAL-mah-PEET-ah).

FAXON YUCCA *Yucca faxoniana* Sarg.
  Leaves as in the last species but *dark green* and *smooth-surfaced.* Flower clusters *3'- 4'* long. In this species and the next, flower segments are *united at the base to form a tube* which, in this species, is *1/2"* long. To 15' tall. Desert scrub. Found in far w. Texas and locally in adjacent Coahuila, Mexico. Hybridizes with Torrey Yucca. Charles Faxon was an early botanical artist.

CARNEROS YUCCA *Yucca carnerosana* (Trel.) McKelvey
  Leaves *yellow-green;* otherwise as in the preceding species. Blossom cluster *5'- 7'* tall, *nearly as wide as tall.* Flower parts *united for 1".* Height to 20', mainly not branched. A tree of Brewster and Culberson counties, w. Texas, and n. Mexico. Rocky slopes. First found at Carneros Pass, Coahuila, Mexico.

SCHOTT YUCCA *Yucca schottii* Engelm.
  Leaves mostly *1 1/2'– 3'* long, *1"– 2"* wide, blue-green, edges smooth *without* separating fibers. Flower clusters 1'- 3' tall, each flower 1"- 2" long, the stalk *densely hairy,* July–September. Fruits 3"-5" long, *fleshy,* eventually drooping. Height to 15 ft. Wooded canyons and open forests of se. Arizona /sw. New Mexico and adjacent Mexico at 4000–7000 ft. elevations. Also known as Hoary Yucca and Mountain Yucca. Arthur Schott, a 19th-century botanist of German birth, found the species during the United States-Mexico Boundary Survey.

BEAKED YUCCA *Yucca rostrata* Engelm. ex Trel.
  Leaves only *15"- 24"* long, *3/8"–1/2"* wide, yellow-green, *flat* above, ± keeled, the edges mostly *fine-toothed.* Flowers *not* united. Like Soaptree Yucca (Plate 40), fruits erect, *dry, splitting open,* ± numerous, 2"- 3" long, with narrow beaks 1"- 1 1/2" long. Height to 15'. Brewster Co., Texas and adjacent Mexico.

[1] See footnote Plate 35.

92

Plate 41

YUCCAS II

	Leaves more than two feet long	Leaves more than two inches wide	Leaf edges showing free fibers	Top of leaves flat /concave	Leaves shade of green[1]	Length of flower stalk in feet	Single blossom more than two inches[2] long
Torrey Yucca	+	+	+	C	G	3-4	+
Faxon Yucca	+	+	+	C	D	3-4	+
Carneros Yucca	+	+	+	C	Y	5-7	+
Schott Yucca	±	±	-	C	B	1-3	-
Beaked Yucca	-	-	-	F	Y	1-4	-

[1] B = blue-, D = dark-, G= Gray-, Y = yellow-green

[2] 0   1"   2"

42. PALMS AND CACTI

In s. Arizona and n. Mexico, these *evergreen* species have either large, parallel-veined leaf fronds or succulent, thorny foliage joints.

CALIFORNIA WASHINGTONIA

Washingtonia filifera (Linden ex Andre) H. Wendl.

A tall palm with *fanlike* leaf fronds *3'- 6'* in diameter, divided into numerous segments that are often much torn and with many loose fibers. The 3'- 6' long leafstalks penetrate the leaf to some degree and bear *hooked thorns*. The trunk is normally covered with dead leaf fronds. Flowers are small, in branched clusters, within a 1'- 2' long, yellowish, narrow spathe, June. Fruits are 1/4"- 1/2" fleshy spheres, black when mature. Height to 50' (75'). Desert waterholes, s. California and Kofa Mountains, sw. Arizona, south into Mexico.

DATE PALM *Phoenix dactylifera* L.

As an example of a *feather-leaved* palm, this cultivated species has *gray-green* leaves 15'- 20' in length, ± *upright,* with the stalk *thornless* and extending the full length of the frond. The Canary Islands Date Palm (*P. canariensis* Chaub.), a landscape species, is a close relative with leaves *light green* and *more drooping.*

SAGUARO (GIANT CACTUS)

Carnegiea gigantea (Engelm.) Britton & Rose

This symbol of the Sonoran desert has a tall, *thorny, green, ribbed* trunk that is *branched* when mature. Flowers white, ± 2" wide, open only about 24 hours, April-May. Fruits fleshy, red, edible, 2"- 3" long, with black seeds, June-July. Height 20'-35' (50'). Rocky soils, se. California and w-cen. Arizona to nw. Mexico. Pronounced sah-WAHR-oh. Trunk swells and becomes smooth after rainfall. The name honors Andrew Carnegie, philanthropist. Formerly *Cereus giganteus* Engelm.

ORGANPIPE CACTUS *Stenocereus thurberi* (Engelm.) F. Buxbaum

With many stems and often sub-upright, this species may not strictly be a tree. Its many slim ribbed branches, however, may be 20' tall. Flowers purplish, May. Dry sites, sw. California and s. Arizona to Sonora, Mexico. Earlier: *Cereus thurberi* Engelm.

JUMPING CHOLLA *Opuntia fulgida* Engelm.

A plant with ± *cylindrical* pads covered with numerous *slender, sharp, barbed* thorns. Flowers pink, ± 1" wide, summer; fruits green, smooth, pear-shaped, without thorns, often in chains. Height to 15'. From cen. Arizona to nw. Mexico. Pronounced CHOY-ya. The plant doesn't jump, but *you* will if you brush against the harpoonlike spines! Joints break off and take root. Fruits eaten by rodents, deer, and javelinas. Rodents and birds nest in the branches. Known also as Chainfruit Cholla.

Plate 42

CALIFORNIA
WASHINGTONIA

DATE PALM

SAGUARO

ORGANPIPE
CACTUS

JUMPING
CHOLLA

KEY TO LEAFLESS TREES

Each key item is a couplet. Compare the unknown specimen with the first pair of choices. Select the alternative that agrees with the specimen and proceed to the couplet number indicated. Repeat until a final determination is reached. Use a lens when necessary.

1. *Leaf scars opposite* (Sections II and III of text). **2**
1. Leaf scars alternate (Sections IV and V of text) **10**

   2. Leaf scars meeting in raised points.   **Ashleaf Maple Pl. 9**
   2. Leaf scars not meeting in raised points. **3**

3. Buds without scales, hairy, opposite mostly only near
   twig tips.   **Birchleaf Buckthorn Pl. 36**
3. Buds with two or more scales, smooth-granular in ashes. **4**

   4. Twigs silvery, ± thorn-tipped; bundle scar 1.
      Silver Buffaloberry Pl. 12
   4. Twigs otherwise; bundle scars various. **5.**

5. Twigs stout; pith wide; central end bud missing, a single pair
   of buds usually present at twig tips.   **Elderberries Pl. 8**
5. Twigs slender; pith narrow; central end bud present, often
   flanked by side buds. **6**

   6. Bud scales two. **7**
   6. Bud scales several. **8**

7. Twigs brown, pith tan.   **Western Mountain Maple Pl. 11**
7. Twigs red to purple, pith white.   **Red-osier Dogwood Pl. 12**

   8. Bundle scar one.   **Buttonbush, Forestiera Pl. 12**
   8. Bundles scars three or more per leaf scar. **9**

9. Buds smooth, granular; fruits single-winged.   **Ashes Pls. 9, 10**
9. Bud scales obvious; fruits in winged pairs.

      Canyon Maple Pl. 11

   10. *Leaf scars alternate, thorns present.* **11**
   10. *Leaf scars alternate,* thorns absent. **16**

11. Thorns paired. **12**
11. Thorns single. **13**

   12. Spur branches lacking.   **Locusts Pl. 13**
   12. Spur branches present.   **Mesquites, etc. Pl. 14**

13. Twigs spine-tipped.   **Leafless Desert Trees Pls. 21;**
      Desert Apricot, Bitter Condalia Pl. 22
13. Twigs not spine-tipped, side thorns spiny or spurlike (see also
   Littleleaf Sumac Pl. 18 and Russian-olive Pl. 33 ± thorny). **14**

   14. Thorns curved, hooked.   **Catclaws Pl. 15**
   14. Thorns more or less straight. **15**

15. Temperate-zone trees spiny or with spur branches more or less thorny, flowers roselike, fruits juicy.
Hawthorns, American Plum Pl. 22
15. Arid-zone trees spiny, flowers pealike, fruits pea-pods.
SW. Coralbean Pl. 13, Blue Paloverde , etc. Pl. 15

16. *Thornless trees* lacking unique (a-i) characteristics. **17**
16. *Thornless trees with unique (a-i) characteristics:*
   a. Leaf scars distinctly 3-lobed, buds dark, bundle scars many. **Mexican-buckeye Pl. 16**
   b. Leaf scars 1/4"- 3/4" deep, triangular; twigs thick, pith solid, bundle scars many. **Tree-of-Heaven Pl. 17**
   c. Trunk bark mottled, flaky; leaf scars O-shaped, surrounding buds; twigs ringed; buds with a single scale.
Sycamore Pl. 23
   d. Pith chambered or at least blocked at the nodes.
Walnuts Pl. 16, Netleaf Hackberry Pl. 24
   e. Buds clustered at the twig tips, acorn fruits.
Oaks Pls. 26-29
   f. Buds with a single, smooth, mostly caplike scale but trees otherwise unlike Sycamore above. **Willows Pls. 30-32**
   g. Twigs silvery, ± thorny. **Russian-olive Pl. 33**
   h. Catkins like inch-long pine cones, usually present; buds blunt with 2-3 scales not overlapping. **Alders Pl. 34**
   i. Buds without scales. **Birchleaf Buckthorn Pl. 36**

17. Leaf scars U-shaped, more or less surrounding the buds.**18**
17. Leaf scars otherwise. **19**

18. Fruits small, dry, clustered, red-hairy, pith wide, twigs often flat-sided, bundle scars many.
Sumacs Pls. 16, 17, 18
18. Fruits dry, circular, winged, brown; pith narrow; twigs rounded; bundle scars 3. **Common Hoptree Pl. 17**

19. Buds with lowermost scale centered directly above the leaf scar; bark often smooth and greenish on young trunk and branches; spur branches occasional. **Poplars Pl. 25**
19. Bud scales and trunk bark otherwise. **20**

20. Trunk bark peeling. **Western Kidneywood, etc. Pl.18**
20. Trunk bark not peeling. **21**

21. Bundle scar one.
Desert-willow, Jumping-bean Sapium Pl. 33
21. Bundle scars three or more. **22**

22. Inner bark of small branches can be pulled in strong fibrous strips when cut. **23**
22. Inner bark weak, not especially fibrous. **24**

23. Bundle scars three; sap clear; buds dark; fruits small, dry, circular. **Siberian Elm Pl. 37**
23. Bundle scars four or more; sap milky (if not too cold); buds reddish; fruits blackberrylike. **Mulberries Pl.23**

24. *Spur branches* lacking. **25**
24. *Spur branches* usually present (see also Poplars Pl. 25). **27**

25. Leaf scars triangular or three-lobed, buds small, often imbedded. **Western Soapberry Pl. 17**
25. Leaf scars ± crescent-shaped, buds large not imbedded. **26**

26. Two or three lines descend from leaf scars on vigorous twigs, fruits dry pea-pods. **California Redbud Pl. 24**
26. Such lines lacking, fruits catkins.
Knowlton Hornbeam Pl. 34

27. Trunk marked with short horizontal lines; fruits one-seeded, dry or fleshy. **28**
27. Trunk bark without horizontal lines; buds long-pointed, scales often twisted and with black notched tips, second bud scale ± half length of bud; fruits several-seeded, fleshy, purple.
Juneberry, Serviceberry Pl. 36

28. Buds with 2-3 scales; broken twigs without an almond or sour odor; fruits dry catkins (see Mountain Alder, Pl. 34).
Water Birch Pl. 34
28. Buds with 4-6 scales; broken twigs often with an almond or sour odor; fruits juicy spheres. **Cherries Pl. 35**

REFERENCES

Argus, George W. 1995. *Salicaceae: Willow Family, Part Two: Salix.* Journ. Arizona-Nevada Acad. Sci. 29 (1): 39-52.

Baerg, Harry J. 1973. *The Western Trees. 2nd ed.* W. C. Brown Co.: Dubuque, Iowa.

Benson, Lyman and Robert A. Darrow. 1954. *Trees and Shrubs of the Southwestern Deserts.* 2nd ed. Tucson: Univ. Arizona Press and Albuquerque: Univ. New Mexico Press.

Berry, James Berthold. 1966. *Western Forest Trees.* Dover Publ., New York.

Elias, Thomas S. 1980. *The Complete Trees of North America.* New York: Van Rostrand Reinhold.

Elmore, Francis H. and Jeanne R. Janish. 1976. *Shrubs and Trees of the Southwest Uplands.* Southwest Parks and Monuments Asso., Tucson.

Fowells, H.A. 1965. *Silvics of Forest Trees of the United States.* U.S. Dept. Agric. Forest Service. Agric. Handbook 271.

Hickman, James C. (edit.) 1993. *The Jepson Manual: Higher Plants of California.* Berkeley, Univ. Calif. Press.

Kearney, Thomas H. and Robert H. Peebles. 1969. *Arizona Flora.* Berkeley: Univ. California Press.

Lamb, Samuel H. 1977. *Woody Plants of the Southwest.* Santa Fe, New Mexico: Sunstone Press.

Landrum, Leslie R. 1992. *Sapotaceae: Sapodilla Family.* Journ. Arizona-Nevada Acad. Sci. 26 (1): 34-35.

-------------1994. *Fagaceae: Oak Family.* Journ. Arizona-Nevada Acad. Sci. 27 (2): 203-214.

------------ 1995. *Aceraceae: Maple Family.* Journ. Arizona-Nevada Acad. Sci. 29 (1): 2-5.

Little, Elbert L., Jr. 1971. *Atlas of United States Trees. Vol. 1: Conifers and Important Hardwoods.* Washington: U.S. Dept. Agriculture Misc. Publ. 1146.

------------1976. *Atlas of United States Trees. Vol. 3:* Minor Western Hardwoods. Washington: U.S. Dept. Agric. Misc. Publ.1314

-----------1979. *Checklist of United States Trees.* U.S Forest Service, Department of Agriculture, Agric. Handbook 541.

-----------1980. *The Audubon Society Field Guide to North American Trees: Western Region.* New York: Alfred A. Knopf.

MacMahon, James A. 1988. *Warm Deserts* in North American Terrestrial Vegetation. Cambridge Univ. Press, New York.

McDougall, W.B. and Omer E. Sperry. 1951. *Plants of the Big Bend National Park.* U.S. Department of the Interior, National Park Service, Washington.

Morin, Nancy R. (edit.). 1993, 1997. *Flora of North America,* vols. 2 and 3. New York, Oxford, Oxford Univ. Press.

Petrides, George A. and Olivia Petrides. 1992, 1998. *A Field Guide to Western Trees.* Houghton Mifflin Co., Boston.

-----------1999. *Trees of the Rocky Mountains and Intermountain West.* Explorer Press, Williamston, Michigan.

Pinkara, Donald J. 1995. *Cactaceae, Part I: Cactus Family.* Journ. Arizona-Nevada Acad. Sci. 29 (1): 6-12.

Preston, Richard J., Jr. 1940. *Rocky Mountain Trees.* Ames, Iowa: Iowa State Univ. Press.

Texas Forest Service. 1963. *Forest Trees of Texas: How to Know Them.* Bull. 20. College Station, Texas.

Trelease, William. 1967. *Winter Botany.* New York: Dover (reprint of 3rd ed., 1931).

Wauer, Roland H. 1980. *Naturalist's Big Bend.* Texas A. & M. Univ. Press. College Station and London.

Wooton, E.O and Paul C. Standley. 1972. *Flora of New Mexico.* Reprints of U.S. Floras. New York: Wheldon & Wesley, Ltd.

INDEX TO PLATES

1. Joshuatree Yuccas and Cholla Cacti, Joshua Tree National Park, Calif.
2. Saguaro and Organpipe cacti, Organpipe National Park, Arizona.
3. Canyon Trail, Chiricahua National Monument, Arizona.

1.Saguaro, Saguaro National Monument, Arizona.
  2. Saguaro trunk thorny, green, ribbed; smooth after rains.
3. Soaptree Yucca, near Willcox, Arizona.
  4. Elephant-tree, Desert Botanical Garden, Phoenix, Arizona.

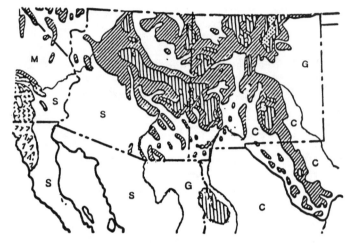

FOREST TYPES and CHAPARRAL -

      SPRUCE - FIR

      PONDEROSA PINE - DOUGLAS FIR

      PINYON - JUNIPER

      CHAPARRAL

CREOSOTE-BUSH* DESERTS and GRASSLANDS -

      M = MOHAVE

      S = SONORAN

      C = CHIHUAHUAN

      G = GRASSLANDS

*Creosote-bush [*Larrea tridentata* (DC.) Cov.], a shrub whose tiny leaves have a creosote odor.

   - Adapted from maps of Fowells (1965) and MacMahon (1988).

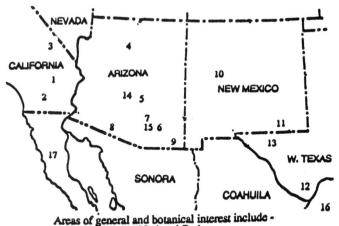

Areas of general and botanical interest include -
1. Joshuatree National Park
2. Anza Borrego Desert State Park
3. Death Valley National Monument
4. Grand Canyon National Park
5. Boyce Thompson Arboretum State Park
6. Saguaro National Park
7. Desert Museum
8. Organpipe Cactus National Monument
9. Chiricahua National Monument
10. Bosque del Apache National Wildlife Refuge
11. Carlsbad Caverns National Park
12. Big Bend National Park
13. Guadalupe National Park
14. Phoenix Botanical Garden
15. Tucson Botanical Garden
16. Chihuahua (Mexican state)
17. Baja California (Mexican state)

INCHES

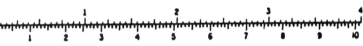

CENTIMETERS

NOTES

NOTES

   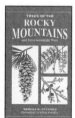